S0-AEC-241

Innovative Human Resource Management

Innovative Human Resource Management

Robert L. Desatnick

AMERICAN MANAGEMENT ASSOCIATION

International standard book number: 0-8144-5264-7
Library of Congress catalog card number: 76-179641

First printing

Preface

The human beings in an organization are its most important resource. Most executives agree, yet there seems to be a wide gap between what we say and the results we accomplish in managing this resource. A recent survey of approximately 100 senior executives points up the widespread continuing concern for people problems. The key items: (1) obtaining good people; (2) utilizing them; (3) motivating them; (4) developing them; (5) compensating them; (6) retaining them.

This book seeks to relate people problems to the realization of corporate objectives, and it provides management tools which can be used to reduce the waste of human resources and to increase the realization of both corporate and personal rewards. It provides a how-to approach, spelling out the role of the human resources executive as initiator and catalyst—in contrast to the often reactive approach of conventional personnel administration. Many illustrations, drawn from actual corporate experience, have been included.

Top management properly demands a high degree of professionalism from its employee relations managers. In doing so, it incurs a related responsibility for selecting, developing, compensating, and supporting these executives at a level appropriate to the professionalism demanded both by management and by the job itself. The characteristics and requirements of the position of chief human resources executive are carefully spelled out.

It is hoped that this book will help senior management, including employee relations executives, to recognize that employee needs, interests, and desires can be harmonized with corporate objectives and to use this knowledge in such a way as to meet the expectations of the corporation and its employees.

Robert L. Desatnick

Contents

Innovative Human Resource Management

1
Our Most Valuable Asset

Chief executives speak of the human resource as the company's most valuable asset. Top management finds itself dealing more and more with people problems. Presidents say they feel more and more like personnel managers because so many of their decisions and so many of the demands on their time have to do with people. Most of the respondents in key manager surveys point to poor human resource management as the primary cause of underachievement. The great majority of executive failures result from ineffective interpersonal relationships, with emphasis on a lack of leadership skills traceable to the inability to manage human resources.

In a recent survey of approximately 100 senior management people, the key concerns reflected by the overwhelming majority of respondents were recruitment, development, utilization, compensation, motivation, and retention of human resources. Not technical or financial problems. People problems. The main issue to be resolved is how to do these things well; at the same time provide for continually increasing productivity, profitability, and growth; and avoid catastrophe. What our senior management people are saying is shown graphically in Exhibit 1-1.

Management concerns are put into perspective in the human resource management system shown in Exhibit 1-1. At the very center of the system—and at the root of most performance failures—are the employee relations policies, objectives, and practices of management. Most managers consider themselves expert in human resource management, yet in many instances the contrary is true.

Employee relations management is a highly complex professional discipline; it can be learned, but there must be someone to teach it. The system in Exhibit 1-1 shows the interrelationship among the most essential aspects of human resources management. While top management usually sees them as separate concerns, they are actually inseparable in good employee relations practice because managerial pro-

Exhibit 1-1.
HUMAN RESOURCE MANAGEMENT FOR PROFIT AND GROWTH

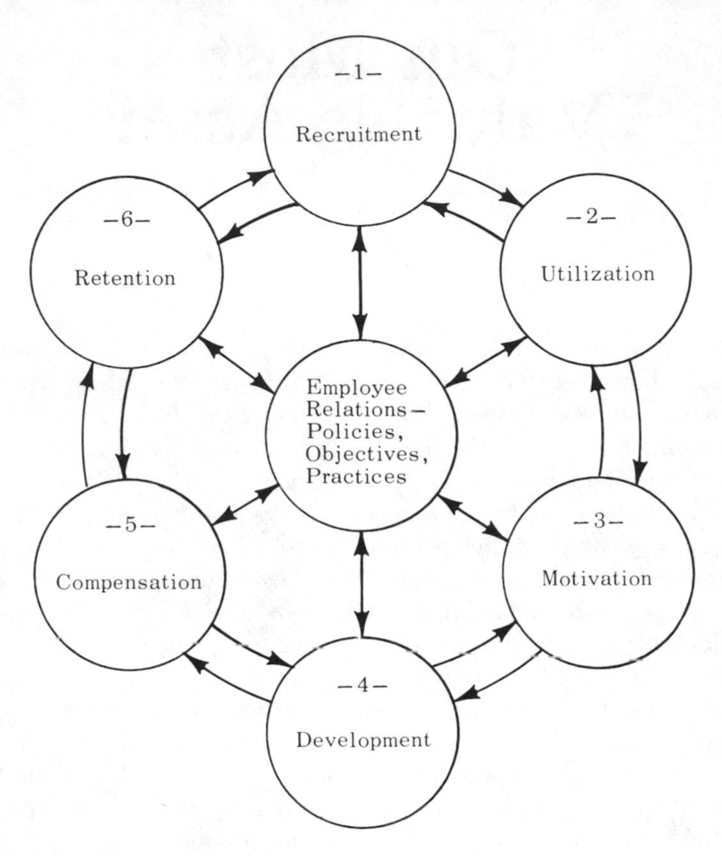

ficiency in one area vitally affects and is affected by proficiency or the lack of it in other areas. To put it another way, these keys to good employee relations management are also keys to the realization of most of management's objectives.

For example, *recruitment* of good people is the result of a carefully planned sequence of events which begins with the establishment of a clear direction for the business. It includes effective business planning, organization planning, and manpower planning. Candidates today, especially for executive positions, are highly sophisticated. They are better educated and more self-confident than the candidates of the past. They quickly sense whether the company has direction and purpose. They look to see how the open position fits into the company's overall business plan and what they are expected to contribute. In the absence of clearly defined position responsibilities, candidates become uneasy. Specifically, business planning is deficient if it neglects systematic manpower planning. Business plans which limit themselves to considerations of land, brick and mortar, facilities, equipment, machinery, processing, products, and markets are predestined for trouble. This is one of the major reasons for today's manager manpower crisis. We have neglected to plan for and develop the men who would make the plans work.

Similarly, organization planning is also a means to an end. Effective organization plans serve to create a framework of working relationships by providing clearly defined responsibilities. Good organization helps to eliminate confusion, duplication, and overlapping of effort. It contributes to increased profitability, reduced expenses, improved job performance, and more effective utilization of human resources.

Effective business and organization plans improve selection because position requirements are directly related to the jobs that need to be filled before business plans and objectives can be realized. It takes good people to make good business plans as well as to make the plans work. Many of management's problems could be screened out at the employment office by screening in good people. To hire the best possible salaried candidates requires:

1. Effective business planning, organization planning, and manpower planning.
2. Clear, concise organizational objectives.
3. A climate conducive to individual development.
4. Promotional opportunity.
5. Enlightened up-to-date personnel policies, including provision for relocation costs, salary administration, and management participation, properly implemented and maintained.
6. Development of manpower sources such as search firms and development of good community relationships and corporate image, reputation, and citizenship—for organizations large or small—because of the importance of these factors in attracting good people.
7. Well-defined position descriptions.
8. Specific performance standards for each position.
9. Carefully developed personnel specifications.
10. Interviewing skills by all managers who make hiring decisions.
11. Appropriate reference checking.
12. Competitive compensation and benefits packages.

If organizations were to rate themselves on each of these factors, all would find room for improvement. Therefore, each must accentuate the positive. Find out where the strengths lie and use those actively in the recruitment, advertising, and interviewing processes. Interviewing skills can be taught and managers can significantly improve their batting averages (ratio of hires to offers extended). Each of these 12 considerations is explored in detail and specific examples are included in Chapter 6.

If a good job has been done in recruitment, chances are that a good job will also be done in *utilization,* the second key to the attainment of management objectives. Surveys show that most managers consider themselves underutilized, and quite often they are. When a man is recruited for a specific job which needs to be done to realize broad organizational objectives, and this is translated into a work plan for the first year, the chances of full utilization are excellent. Couple this with a specification of priorities and action plans agreed upon by man and manager, and executives will be properly utilized.

In actual practice this is more likely to happen: The position is loosely defined, and senior executives really never agree as to what the position should contribute to organization goals. A good man is found and hired not because he will fit the job but because he will adapt and make his way. Consequently, he becomes a wart on the organization; he has no real goals and hence no plan that will link his efforts with those of other executives. He spends more time in defensive maneuvering than in constructive job accomplishment. He ends up being underutilized.

Companies and institutions cannot organize and staff for the periods of peak activity; it would be too expensive to do so. What actually happens is that organizations are lean in some periods and heavy in others. The human resources executive should take the lead in identifying real manpower needs and comparing them with existing human resources. He has to draw up a detailed manpower inventory record on each employee, with special emphasis on exempt salaried employees. As special situations require special skills, a task force can be made up from the inventory, which would include the specific skills and knowledge deemed to be needed to produce results.

Effective manpower utilization is also an excellent form of expense control. Often people are assigned responsibilities for which they are overqualified. In the absence of good systematic job evaluation and salary administration practices, there is a tendency to pay more dollars than the job is worth instead of reassigning the incumbent to a position requiring his higher skills. Often, responsibilities can be added to an individual's position without tampering with the organization structure and without an increase in salary costs. Many positions, for example, do not require college training, and hiring college graduates to fill them not only contributes to higher turnover because of boredom and lack of challenge, but compels the company to pay a premium to get the work done. To avoid this, the real requirements for the job must be defined.

Another effective technique for determining the degree of human resource utilization is to have every manager review the contribution of each exempt employee reporting directly to him—not only performance, but also position in the organization structure, compensation, age, health, and potential for advancement. Each manager should then be asked to identify the top 10 percent and the bottom 10 percent of performers in terms of effectiveness. As part of his action plan for people utilization, his next step would be to develop appropriate plans for each individual in these two groups.

To improve utilization of the top group, a number of alternatives—job enlargement, special assignment, tougher objectives, promotion, salary increase, task force assignment—could be appropriate. In any event, a special accelerated approach should be tailored for each individual.

In the bottom group, improvement in job perfomance is the primary consideration. Specific performance targets and standards must be spelled out, along with timing. Failure to meet these standards should result in demotion, salary reduction, early retirement, or termination. No organization can remain vital if it continues to tolerate mediocre or unsatisfactory performance. Obsolescence of skills or reduced output impairs effective utilization of human resources throughout the organization.

Manpower planning in its broadest sense encompasses manpower utilization and manpower development. Traditionally, personnel people have been concerned with day-to-day clerical operations and routines involved in hiring, transferring, and laying off people, filling out forms, and explaining the benefit package. They responded to requests and paid little heed to their potential contribution to the success and profitability of the business.

Today, the human resources executive should have immediately available to him a survey of the organization's human resources in depth. This should be in the form of a manpower inventory that details each employee's education, experience, specialized training, accomplishments, salary history, and career interests, as well as performance appraisals and ratings of promotability and potential. The manager utilizes his resources by matching up manpower availability and current and anticipated needs with regard to plant expansion, new markets, new technology, changing business conditions, and governmental and labor relations.

The employee relations people should still perform the traditional recruiting, interviewing, and placement functions, but there is much room for innovation even in these areas. With systematic manpower planning, manager development can be set up to go on continually and not be curtailed in bad times. The commitment by top management to such a program will help to insure a supply of qualified replacements for jobs vacated by planned transfers and promotions.

There are other dimensions to manpower planning. In recent years we have become very much aware of how difficult it is to increase productivity through better utilization of people and through creating an organizational environment in which people put forth their best efforts. We are now reaching the point where additional gains in productivity will come about through improved manpower utilization as opposed to facilities modernization and technological development. In other words, increased output at all organizational levels is more likely to result from effective human resource management than from improved equipment.

Improvements in workforce utilization depend to a large degree on top-level support, understanding, and cooperation. To illustrate what it takes to get information about an organization's human resources, a durable goods manufacturer employing 7,000 people spent two years computerizing an employee records system into a master employee relations file. But the resultant manpower dynamics pointed up quantitatively and qualitatively the organization's manpower situation. It told the who, when, why, and how of hirings, promotions, transfers, and terminations; and it included age of the workforce, critical managerial and factory skills, benefits, and participation. It helped to develop policies and priorities aimed at improving manpower utilization. It sold management on the need for three skilled apprentice programs. It opened the doors to systematic recruiting of management trainees to fill exempt positions in advance of permanent openings. Managers never cease to be amazed at how quickly normal attrition can deplete managerial resources and key skills at nonexempt salaried and hourly levels.

While companies carefully plan to capture new markets, build new plants, and develop growth strategies, few clearly spell out their manpower requirements. In recent years, for example, two large companies planned to bring new plants on stream three years in advance of production. Both plants were abandoned subsequently because of an inability to attract people to work in them. If the manpower budget is made an integral part of the total planning process, the numbers and kinds of jobs to be filled can be forecast, and existing skills can be more effectively utilized. A business climate survey can also provide valuable assistance.

Effective utilization of executive talent can reduce the need for additional executives. One technique has been to reorganize the business to minimize the number of executives needed for effective management. This can be done by combining operations with common markets and/or common technology or by combining two smaller operations with geographic proximity. The best executives are retained, salary costs are reduced, and the executives are further challenged through broadened multiplant, multiproduct responsibilities. The same technique can be effected by combining jobs after careful study of the contribution of two like positions to an organization's objectives.

An exceptional engineering manager in a large consumer durable goods manufacturing company has a staff of six design engineers whose average annual compensation is $18,000 per year. His colleagues have 12 to 18 design engineers in similar situations, but their pay ranges from $14,000 to $17,000 per year. The manager with the smaller staff has a record of exceptional performance from his group—and his people are frequently chosen for promotion. Thus quality can be an overriding factor in the right situation.

Decentralization, while a fine concept, can result in major personnel and profit problems. The changeover can be expensive, and care must be taken to insure that the activities to be decentralized are not decontrolled. Periodically, the human resources executive should audit line and staff activities to determine not only who is doing what, and when, and why, but whether it should be done at all. Are the most effective working relationships established? Is the work more properly done by line or staff people? What is the degree of overlap or duplication? Besides clearing the air for more effective communication, the executive can identify work which should be eliminated as well as work which needs to be done and is not being done, and he can assess the effects of both situations on business results. This is another excellent technique to modernize utilization of human resources.

As more responsibilities are shifted to fewer executives, it is easier to measure the actual contribution of each and minimize buck-passing. Since the contributions are easier to measure, the compensation problems become simpler. As a case in point, one large food chain has no published organization charts or position descriptions. The stated reason is "to keep from stifling individual initiative and growth." But this firm has run into difficulties in trying to broaden its young managerial group because compensation and status problems have made certain transfers prohibitive. This is at least in part because permanent positions have fixed salary ranges despite the lack of a clearly defined organizational hierarchy. Freedom of expression and the opportunity to contribute are not best realized in a largely unstructured situation, particularly in a big company. While there is a great deal of merit in an individual-centered approach to organization, much more work must be done by behavioral scientists before this concept can be proved in practice.

The behavioral sciences focus much of their attention on the behavior of men in social settings, of which the industrial environment is one. The purpose is to find out how people react to given conditions and, having analyzed the conditions that produce desirable and undesirable behavior, apply these findings to create an organizational setting that serves to motivate—to produce desirable behavior. The orientation is toward the realization of personal and economic objectives through a variety of practices and techniques such as management by objectives, about which more will be said later.

This book concerns itself with applications of behavioral research principles and findings to every manager's job. It is commonplace in business to hire managerial trainees, only to have half of them leave within two years. A close scrutiny of the reasons for leaving points strongly to inadequate utilization as one of the main causes. Each trainee really wants to earn his salary and not sit at someone's elbow for one to three years before he can make his contribution. Each wants and needs a chance to succeed or fail. One machine tool manufacturer realized this and made the recruitment job easier as well as significantly reducing turnover. Managers were not permitted to have a trainee unless they submitted a carefully thought-out project to the human resources executive. Such a project had to be measurable; it had to last six months to a year; and it had to solve a real management problem—poor quality control, high turnover, excessive inventory, design change, or implementation of an interdepartmental communication system. Some guidelines for management trainee utilization are shown in Exhibit 1-2.

The key factors that affect the utilization of human resources also affect recruitment. Thus an interesting, meaningful pattern of relationships begins to emerge. Whatever it takes to bring good people into the organization also plays a predominant role in utilizing those same people. The business practices and tools that are valid and useful in the one situation are equally valid and useful in the other. This is the reason for the model on human resources management in Exhibit 1-1. Good human resources management is not a series of isolated, unrelated business and personnel practices, but is instead a closely interrelated network of effective practices focused on an organization's human resources.

Thus *motivation*, in the third circle of our model, is similarly affected by good and by bad management practice. Perhaps the greatest waste in today's society is a waste of our human resources. The sad fact is that the cause is not the employee's lack of ability or willingness to perform. Rather, it is management's failure to realize that most people really want to do a good job and do not need to be coerced or enticed into doing so. The late Douglas McGregor, regarded as one of the foremost behavioral scientists, shot into national prominence with his theory X and theory Y, two differing views on the nature of man in relation to his work.

Theory X was predicated on assumptions such as these: People naturally dislike work and will avoid it if at all possible; they must be coerced, threatened, controlled, directed to contribute to organizational goals; they actually want to avoid responsibility, prefer to be directed, and have very little ambition. When management adopts this philosophy at any organizational level, the results are restricted output, passive resistance, disloyalty, and militant unionism. This management style displays no awareness of the real contributors to human motivation. The result is autocratic or dictatorial management with as little communication as possible—upward, downward, or sideways. The individual never sees the broad picture, never appreciates his contribution to the team effort.

Theory Y, on the other hand, involves a different set of assumptions about people. Theory Y assumes that people naturally expend mental and physical energy in performing productive work; they are basically self-directed and willingly exert themselves to attain organization goals if they are committed as a result of receiving satisfactions from the work—pay, recognition, a sense of achievement. People can and will learn to accept responsibility, according to theory Y; they are inherently creative and capable of exercising a high degree of imagination and ingenuity toward solving work-related problems; and, under present business conditions, they are permitted to use just a small part of what they are potentially able to contribute.

Acceptance of McGregor's cogent analysis of management styles led to a revolution in management. It fostered delegation of responsibility, provided the genesis for goal-oriented management, aided decentralization as an organizational concept, and facilitated a boom in communication. Managers began to realize that a job could be satisfying and rewarding and yet contribute significantly to business goals if people were treated as valuable assets.

As a negative example, one company president, because of the pressures of the marketplace and rising costs, decided to subscribe to the new theories of motivation, so he began to hold regular weekly staff meetings for the first time. The idea was good, but the implementation left a great deal to be desired. He told everybody on his staff what

Exhibit 1-2.
TRAINING PROGRAM FOR MANAGEMENT TRAINEES

Responsibility of Assignment Supervisor

Each management trainee must be provided with an assignment sufficiently challenging to make him—

1. Earn his salary.
2. Make a real contribution.
3. Acquire broad knowledge about the function within which he is working.

In order to attract and retain the caliber of men we need for continued growth and progress, each assignment must be carefully planned.

Evaluation of Performance

Upon completion of a training assignment in the manager's function, the trainee will be evaluated on the attached form. It should be noted that evaluation of performance is a continuing process directed toward improving an individual's contribution to the business and increasing his effectiveness.

At the outset of his assignment, the trainee should be told in detail the areas for which he will be held accountable, including results to be obtained. Only in this way can we insure maximum utilization of the trainee.

General Information

1. Each trainee will normally spend six months in the program (one-half of each day in his own functional area and one-half on rotating job assignments).
2. The human resources executive will be responsible for the administration of the program, and the trainee will meet with him bimonthly.
3. Each trainee will be expected to perform useful functions from which he can learn while he is doing productive work.
4. Each trainee will be formally evaluated by the supervisor for whom he works immediately following the assignment.
5. A written report is to be submitted by the trainee to the human resources executive at the completion of this program. The report should include the following:
   a. Major points learned.
   b. Projects worked on and assignments of a continuing nature.
   c. Problems encountered.
   d. Suggestions for improvement.
6. Following the training assignment, each trainee will be evaluated on his overall performance and assigned to a regular position based upon his evaluation. Consideration will be given to the interests of the trainee in making the permanent assignment.

Analysis of Factors Affecting Trainee Performance

Complete this analysis before making your overall appraisal of trainee's performance with respect to his accountability factors.

Factors	Comments supporting appraisal	Rating*
1. *Knowledge and skill*		
a. Knowledge of the functions involved.		
b. Knowledge of significantly related functions.		
c. Evidence of additional study for present or future.		
2. *Application of knowledge and skill*		
a. Quality of decisions on normal problems.		
b. Quality of decisions under difficult or unusual conditions.		
c. Extent of origination of new methods, plans, programs.		
d. Effectiveness in using new ideas.		
3. *Results obtained*		
a. Record for meeting normal commitments.		
b. Record for meeting unusual commitments.		
c. Accomplishments in relation to anticipated results.		
d. Record for follow-through under difficult circumstances.		
e. Record for accuracy and thoroughness.		
4. *Attitudes*		
a. Toward suggestions or criticism.		
b. Toward additional responsibility.		
c. Toward the difficult parts of his job.		
5. *Related abilities*		
a. To persuade others orally.		
b. To write clearly and effectively.		
c. To collect and present important facts.		
6. *Capacity to work with others*		
a. Recognition of rights and abilities of others.		
b. Contributions to group thought and action.		
c. Record for obtaining cooperation of others.		
d. Record for meeting requests for help.		

* Outstanding; Excellent; Good; Minimum; Unacceptable.

was shipped during the past week and asked for questions, remarks, or discussion. His attitude for the most part precluded, even stifled, any form of participation. When one member of the management team raised a question involving a delicate problem between sales and manufacturing, the president tabled the matter and effectively cut off present as well as future discussion. The organization continued to flounder and lose market share and miss opportunities.

The point is that a dramatic change overnight is practically impossible for any organization. The important factor is the attitude of the chief executive. If he perceives the need for change and provides the necessary support and assistance, the chief human resources executive can make sure that change for the better is thoroughly conceived, effectively implemented, and permanently implanted.

There are other considerations in the complex of human behavior. Participation and involvement must not be illusory. If the intent is to deceive managers by providing the trappings but not the fact of participation, it becomes manipulation and is self-defeating. People cannot be bought off. Good human relations devolve from strength, not weakness.

Another major contributor to motivation theory was Abraham Maslow. From his early investigations into the nature of motivation, he recognized that motivation comes from within, not from outside forces. We are all goal seekers from the beginning to the end of life, and our drives motivate our behavior. Hence, man converts his goals to needs. These needs are generated from within and begin with basic survival needs—food, shelter—and on up the hierarchy to the need for safety, for belonging and love, for self-respect and recognition of personal worth, and last but most important, the need for self-realization (self-actualization, to use Maslow's word).

All of us want to become what we are capable of becoming. Built into every human being is a desire to release his true potential—to become his true self. A person who is in the process of becoming his true self is self-actualized. He is spontaneous, creative, and capable of tremendous accomplishments—on the job as well as off. A self-actualized person is constantly striving—always reaching out to new goals. Every employer must recognize that once lower-level physical and security needs are fulfilled, other needs replace them, and the former satisfactions no longer serve as motivators.

Recent surveys of executives who changed jobs list money as No. 3 or No. 4 in order of importance; challenge, opportunity, more responsibility were all judged to be more significant. Those men are saying, we no longer perceived ourselves as fulfilling our potential and so we quit to take other jobs that seemed to have greater possibilities for self-actualization. This is a good reason why exit interviews, skillfully conducted by the human resources executive, are so important—to identify whether the organization climate fosters or stifles creative self-expression and individual development and to identify the managers who stifle initiative so their efforts can be redirected. Behavioral science findings have numerous practical implications, all of which involve good management practice.

Frederick Herzberg added further refinements to the practical utilization of motivation theory. Dr. Herzberg centered his attention on satisfaction and dissatisfaction in his study of a group of engineers and accountants. Among other things, he found that the opposite of satisfaction on the job is not dissatisfaction; instead, it is no satisfaction at all. The implications for managers are quite profound.

Among the satisfiers Herzberg identified is *achievement*, or the satisfaction of solving a problem, or getting a job done. Briefly, this means being able to see the results of one's efforts. Achievement is so important that it calls for special consideration. We in industry have prided ourselves on the fact that we can take complex clerical and factory jobs, break them up into relatively simple operations, assign a person to each operation, and precisely measure output. We are also trying to do this with managerial jobs, but have not yet found a way. Such work simplification is not only dehumanizing the work, but in a sense is insulting the individual. No wonder people sometimes cheer when an assembly line breaks down. People need the satisfaction of knowing they have satisfactorily completed a piece of work. Organizations which have started to regroup and enlarge jobs to use people's initiative have reaped huge dividends in terms of increased productivity, improved attendance, and superior quality. Increased loyalty, too, is an important byproduct.

A technically brilliant vice-president of manufacturing once had a large staff of people, but constantly interfered with each man's operations. He would assign a job to a person one day, then reassign it to someone else before it was completed. He never gave the individual the feeling of having satisfactorily completed a job. Sometimes he would step in and finish the job, although his people were perfectly capable of doing it themselves. He robbed them of achievement and in so doing, paid some stiff penalties—including a high turnover rate.

Recognition is another important satisfier. Why managers are reluctant to compliment good work is impossible to understand. Public recognition, properly deserved, sets a high standard for future performance as well as satisfying another one of man's most important needs. It emphasizes the high degree of confidence a manager has in his people; it gives needed feelings of reassurance.

The work itself is a most important contributor to individual motivation. A job can be interesting or boring, challenging or taxing, creative or stifling, easy or difficult. The manager's attitude toward the man and the job is significant here, as is job content. One vice-president of employee relations really believes that the way to keep an executive happy is to keep him busy. Consequently, he loads his people with make-work projects and mundane, boring, mechanistic chores, while he saves the really important jobs for himself. This obsolete concept of motivation has significantly reduced productivity and contributed to relatively high executive turnover.

Executives are not interested in volume for volume's sake; they need work that fully taxes their creative energies and analytical abilities. They need important, rewarding work. Not to provide stimulating work is a major cause of management failure because it contributes to unsatisfactory interpersonal relationships and effectively shuts off communication. Contrast the vice-president of employee relation just mentioned with the human resources executive who challenges his people to come up with meaningful goals that are attainable through improved productivity, costs, market position, and delivery. It is easy to understand where one fails and the other succeeds. Giving people real *responsibility* forms the basis for job enrichment and job enlargement; it means giving a wide latitude of authority, control, and accountability. This permits a man to contribute from the full range of his knowledge and experience; it draws out his potential.

Advancement is a related concept. Most people want to get ahead, and their jobs should be the platforms from which they spring to new heights. Therefore the job must contain developmental types of assignments, opportunities for broadening, and the chance to be considered for promotion. The manager who understands motivation pays serious attention to these matters and therefore does not have time to second-guess his people, finish their work before they can do it themselves, interfere in their operations, or closely control or supervise. A good manager uses his human resources to the full extent of their capabilities and willingness to contribute.

This implies *growth,* another great satisfier. The job and the manager must provide opportunities for personal growth and development. Jobs that do not do so will go begging in the future. It is likely that the job offer of the future will include specified opportunities and plans for an individual's growth and development—in recognition of his needs for new knowledge, skills, and experiences and the organization's need for special skills, abilities, and talents. Education will be part of this package, because an educated employee is a more valuable employee.

Herzberg includes in the category of dissatisfiers such factors as salary, status, the physical environment, organization policy, communication policy, manager's technical competence, and relationships with peers, superiors, and subordinates. These, Herzberg says, are more properly termed maintenance or hygiene factors. They are preventive and environmental factors; it is the satisfiers that act as motivators.

Providing salary, status, and the rest may keep employees from being dissatisfied, at least temporarily, but it does not substitute for the satisfiers; it does not create the conditions which will help to generate real motivation from within. Lower-level needs (dissatisfiers) do not have nearly the impact on an organization's ability to attain its goals as do higher-level needs (satisfiers) such as achievement, recognition, the job itself, and opportunities for development and advancement. Interestingly enough, the *satisfiers cost less*, yet yield far greater returns to an enlightened management.

While organizations give their managers explicit instructions and training in the utilization of physical and material assets such as plants, facilities, money, there is a clear lack of direction for the management of human resources. This is described in Chapter 6, which goes into detail about human resources management. Management has too long reneged on its responsibility to meet the growth needs of employees. There is a tendency to hide behind the fact that all development is self-development, but the truth of the matter is that individual growth and development of potential are dependent on the interaction of man, manager, job, and environment. Management must provide the organization, climate, opportunity, and supervision which encourage and foster development.

When an executive finds that his satisfier needs are not met, if he chooses to remain with the organization he becomes a dropout. He transfers papers from the in-basket to the out-basket. Although he is usually a long-service employee who has made significant contributions in the past, he is not necessarily an old man. He is uncertain, hesitant, fearful. He tends to block innovations and suppress bright young comers. His attitude is negative and he is not likely to take risks. He enjoys the comfort of security, and his operation usually reflects stability; no real swings up or down. A helpful hint to avoid having executives become dropouts is to demand excellence year after year by means of exacting performance standards.

Fear can be positive motivation and in the short run can produce impressive results. But the fear of failure is in opposition to the need for achievement which is a prerequisite for success in a competitive situation. The individual whose primary motivation is a need to achieve is looking for the rewards that accompany success, whereas the fear of failure merely motivates him to avoid the consequences. The manager who is afraid to fail will seek the safe and easy way, choose low-risk situations even though they promise a low return. As an example of fear motivation, the general manager faced with an absolute need to expand first tries to purchase additional goods or services by subcontracting the work at a lesser profit. In the event that this is not possible, he seeks excuses for delay or tries to get people to make his decision for him. Such a man will expand the old plant first, ignoring the basic economic facts, until he is forced to build and staff a new plant operation.

The entrepreneurial manager, on the other hand, actively seeks a job that entails considerable decision making, individual accountability for his decisions, objective feedback of results, and the risk of failure. He welcomes additional responsibility instead of shirking it.

Others also have contributed substantially to our storehouse of information on motivation. Chris Argyris, for example, places high value on the need for frankness, openness, and candor in an organization. He views interpersonal competence as a most significant factor in establishing cohesive work groups. The interaction of a manager with his people and the effect of his leadership style upon the group's motivation and productivity are viewed as highly significant. Argyris is a strong proponent of sensitivity training in human relationships as the answer to the improvement of interpersonal competence.

Rensis Likert is prominent among those who pioneered in motivation studies. From his early investigations into task-oriented versus people-oriented supervision, he has developed several applications of behavioral research principles. Perhaps one of his most significant accomplishments is the "linking pin" theory, which views a manager as a member of two distinct groups. He is the communications link between his superior officers above and those who report to him below. He communicates upward and downward. He represents his people to upper management, and the degree to which he is effective in satisfying their needs is commensurate with the degree of confidence his subordinates have in him and the degree of cooperation they give or withhold. Dr. Likert clearly perceives an organization's human assets in terms of growth and depletion. When good people are hired, growth takes place; when good people leave, depletion takes place. Dr. Likert shares the belief of other behavioral scientists that few organizations ever really tap the full potential of their people.

Robert Blake and Jane Mouton, with their Managerial Grid,® focus on leadership style with a graphic display of the people concerns versus production concerns in a variety of managerial practices. They see these concerns as complementary rather than independent of each other. Too much concern for one is as bad as too little concern for the other. In the ideal situation, they believe, people are committed to work accomplishment by striving for common organizational goals and purposes which engender mutual trust and respect at all organization levels.

The primary job of the manager is to achieve results through others. If his subordinates are not motivated to help him do so, he has failed as a manager. The morale, attitude, motivation, creativity, quality, and productivity of the work team are up to the manager. If the results of the group in these areas do not meet the manager's expectations, it is because he has not provided the climate, conditions, and leadership which encourage his people to give fully and freely of their energies and ideas—to take calculated risks.

No manager will call forth from within himself that longed-for total commitment, nor will he be able to make his full contribution, unless and until—

- His position, including priorities, is clearly defined.
- He knows what constitutes a job well done in terms of specific results.
- He knows what and when he is doing very well.
- He knows where and when he is falling short of his manager's expectations.
- He is made aware of what should be done to correct unsatisfactory results.
- He is made aware of his opportunities for personal and professional growth and development within the organization.
- He knows that his manager recognizes the value of his contribution and will make it known to others.
- He knows the importance of his contribution.
- He feels that his manager wants him to succeed and progress.
- He is shown concrete evidence that there are ample rewards for exceptional performance.

Just as recruitment and utilization are dependent on sound management practice, so is motivation. The job falls back on the manager's shoulders and fits into place in the model of human resources management.

Development, the fourth element in the model shown in Exhibit 1-1, is no exception because developing managerial talent and capability encompasses the first three elements—recruitment, utilization, and motivation. Development is an interactive process involving the man, his manager, his job, and the work environment. All are interdependent and supportive. Developing managers is an integral part of the manager's job. This is not a personnel program, nor is it a personnel function or responsibility. It is part of every manager's line assignment and part of his responsibility to his company, to his people, to his boss, and to himself. One of a manager's key job requirements should be to provide a replacement for himself. He can insure his own promotion if he does so. The days of keeping managers separate from one another with no lateral communication are gone forever. This practice inhibits development.

Development is closely linked with manpower planning and business planning. Clear organization purpose and direction that determine what talents and skills will be needed to meet new demands of technology, marketplace, labor, government, products, growth, and management information also determine what talents and skills are needed to fill projected openings from within.

There are nine minimum criteria for a successful management development effort.

1. Active participation, support, and commitment must come from the most senior members of the management team. Effective manager development does not begin with efforts of the personnel department to convince middle managers that their people must have new skills and knowledge. The company president must get the ball rolling first by formulating and implementing plans for his own backup man and then requesting his managers to do likewise.

2. An organization needs a clear vision of what it wants to be, where it is going, and how it intends to get there. This requires managers who keep pace with constantly changing technology, marketplace, human relationships, organization, communication, information processing and control. The skills and abilities needed must be identified and then must be developed.

3. Managers' responsibilities and authority must be clearly defined. When people understand how they can contribute to the success of the operation, they willingly exert themselves to accomplish goals. Since the best development is on the job, it stands to reason that the clearer the picture a man has of his job, the more he is able to contribute and reach for challenging new goals.

4. A well-defined position description which is action-oriented should suggest goals to be accomplished along with guidelines for defining quantitative performance standards. The degree of improvement or slippage in performance must be formally measured at least once a year for regular employees and twice as frequently for new employees and transferred or promoted employees. Otherwise there is little or no basis for improving performance, identifying and building

on strengths, and programming to fill voids and developmental needs. It was noted earlier that most people want to improve; with accurate measurements, the way to improvement is shown.

5. Feeding back results is also necessary to effect performance improvement and encourage people to reach for and realize more challenging goals. A man's behavior will not change unless he and his manager arrive at parallel conclusions as to the specific areas where improvement is needed and until the man recognizes for himself a need to change. This is the most important part of development, and it is not accomplished in the day-to-day pressures of keeping things going.

Every individual has a right to know how well he is doing, what he is expected to do differently in order to improve, and what he needs to do to insure his growth, development, and promotion. His manager, in turn, is obligated to provide this information in a constructive and positive manner to give the employee recognition and reassurance as well as help him to overcome obstacles to improvement. A management development effort is ineffective without a built-in system of formal performance appraisal.

6. Management by objectives provides the ideal means for achieving individual participation, recognition, and involvement. The behavioral research findings mentioned earlier suggest that these are necessary ingredients in self-actualization. A case study of how management by objectives was implemented in a diversified company is presented in Chapter 5. If a sound performance appraisal is tied in with results-oriented management, both management's need for business results and individual needs for recognition, involvement, and participation are fulfilled simultaneously.

7. Communication is the lubricant which makes the gears of industry mesh effectively and continuously. Studies have demonstrated that effective managers spend up to 80 percent of their time in communication. The chief considerations in effective two-way communication with understanding include:

- The sincerity and integrity of the manager in his relationships with his men, with his peers, and with his superiors.
- What is communicated—the real issues to be resolved—including the problems, opportunities, new developments, forthcoming changes, job priorities, performance results, and areas for improvement.
- Timing of communications. If management communicates only in times of crises, a credibility gap is established which is hard to bridge. Good news and bad news must be communicated in an environment which has built-in provision for self-criticism. Loyalty

is not won two hours before a strike deadline, nor do managers go that extra mile when they first hear of a new contract by reading about it in the local newspaper.

- The example of management. Action speaks louder than words. The best public relations man cannot obtain dedication for a management which has failed its people by not keeping its promises, by giving partial or half-truths, by manipulation.

8. The manager himself is one of the four major factors in the development process. Therefore his attitude, his work habits, his objectivity, his interest in development, and his leadership style—for better or for worse—will stimulate and promote or stifle and discourage self-development.

It is the manager who must provide the conditions for development. He is like the gardener who plants the flower where it can get sunshine and rain; he does not inject fertilizer into the stem of the plant, but places it around the roots where the plant must reach out to it. Similarly, a person must be placed in a job and in an environment which provide the conditions conducive to self-development. Knowledge and opportunity must be made available to him and he must know that they are there where he can exert himself to reach out and get them with the assistance of his manager. The key, obviously, is the manager. It is he who must nurture and foster the man's development. How many of us would have attained our present positions were it not for a manager who took an interest in our development, encouraged us, gave us exposure, and made promotional and educational opportunities available to us?

9. Last but not least among the criteria for a successful management development effort is a competitive compensation program, properly administered. Although compensation is classified as a dissatisfier and will not serve as a motivator per se, its mismanagement has so strong a negative impact that increasing concern has been directed to it. Compensation is tangible recognition for achievement; it represents a form of status; it dictates a man's standard of living; it represents security to many people.

Because so much attention has been devoted to the subject of *compensation*, and because it has been expressed as a critical concern in management surveys, it becomes the fifth element in our model for effective human resources management. And because the major effort has been directed toward compensation for exempt, salaried employees, this will form the basis for our discussion.

Compensation considerations for exempt employees must satisfy a number of management objectives and employee needs. A good plan must recognize the relative value of each individual's contribution as demonstrated through sustained performance. It must first emphasize actual work accomplishment as measured by objective performance appraisal. This will insure full recognition of exceptional performance while avoiding overpayment for performance below established standards. Many companies treat exempt employees as equals in performance and give flat percentage increases across the board to all exempt employees except perhaps a rare few who have surpassed all standards. This practice drives good people out of the company because tangible recognition of accomplishment is lacking. And, because excellent, mediocre, and poor performance are rewarded alike, compensation dollars are wasted.

A good compensation plan also provides for payment of individual salary rates which will attract and retain capable employees who are willing to meet present and future business needs. It should motivate people to want to strive voluntarily and continually to increase their value and contribution to the company. The plan should provide for the determination of an individual's progress through a results-oriented appraisal system. Competent employees should be advanced to positions of greater value. And perhaps most important is the provision for a communication link between man and manager. There must be open and frank discussion of compensation matters affecting every employee.

There is need for a formal plan in all sizable organizations. Systematic position evaluation helps to determine the relative worth of one job as compared with another. Salary structures provide avenues and ladders for advancement, and each position should have a rate range to permit room for growth through salary adjustment as the individual improves his contribution. One point should be noted: There is no effective universal plan of job evaluation, and separate guidelines must be established for exempt and nonexempt positions.

A major prerequisite to an effective evaluation procedure and maintenance of the system is the position description. Position evaluations must be based on position content, the capabilities required to perform the work, and the relative contribution of the position to the success of the business. In determining the relative worth of the job, it must be remembered that it is the position which is being evaluated and not the man assigned to the position. If the ability of an individual exceeds the needs of his position, an effort should be made to reassign him so as to utilize his skills and abilities more fully. Either the man or his manager can write the description, but both need to agree on its content.

Salary decisions should be made by managers who are responsible for the work of employees as long as such decisions are consistent with approved guidelines and appropriate policies and practices, including salary surveys of comparable jobs outside the company.

The company's needs are to attract and retain and motivate employees and, in the process, achieve maximum value from the work for the salary expended. The employee has a right to expect fair and equitable salary treatment, opportunities for deserved advancement, favorable work situations in which his contribution can be maximized, and communication on salary matters affecting him.

Administration of salary is an individual matter on the exempt level. Each salary should be viewed as unique and separate within general guidelines; there should be no force-fitting to predetermined or edicted statistical parameters. Salaries should be reviewed at least annually.

There are a number of considerations involved in individual salary determinations. These include:

1. Performance in relation to predetermined goals or accountability factors of the position.
2. Market trends, both generally and in relation to special skills.
3. Internal salary structure and internal salary relationships.
4. Cost of living, including special geographic considerations.
5. Company policy and budget considerations—although these should not rule out appropriate increases over an extended period of time.
6. The length of time between adjustments, particularly when business conditions have stretched out increases.
7. Promotion, transfer, or demotion.
8. The possibility of losing the individual, weighed against salary costs for his replacement.
9. The individual's present salary in relation to the range for his position.
10. The rate of salary progress for the individual and whether it bears an appropriate relationship with his potential.
11. Improvement in level of performance.
12. Level of performance of the manager's group, particularly in bonus considerations.

Factors which should not be considered in isolation include age, health, timeliness of decisions, amount of supervision required, initiative exercised, personality, amount of effort expended, amount of travel required, amount of formal education, years of experience, loyalty, and size of family. It should be emphasized that these factors are important only insofar as they contribute to the realization of—or failure to meet—quantitative goals and performance standards.

There are numerous compensation plans, most of them made up of some combination of these elements: base salary, profit sharing, bonuses, commissions, stock bonus, stock options, deferred compensation, insurance, savings plans, fringes. What combination is best varies from year to year with the circumstances and the tax laws. A number of good professional consultants are available to help a company select the best plan for its needs.

It must be borne in mind constantly that business effectiveness is directly related to the ingenuity and effort which exempt employees put forth in their work. It is vital that salaries be so administered as to avoid feelings of dissatisfaction about pay. While satisfaction in itself may not provide the motivation for increased productivity, a feeling of dissatisfaction is an inhibiting factor that prevents the full and effective utilization of executive talent.

Compensation is obviously related to *retention*, which is the sixth and last element in our human resources management system as depicted in Exhibit 1-1. The same factors, individually or in combination, which affect profitability and growth also are related to and affect one another. This is illustrated in Exhibit 1-3.

In addition to the many things discussed in the foregoing pages, there are other tools that can be put to use to improve retention and reduce turnover of employees. One such tool is the preemployment check or reference investigation. One time-saving rule is to avoid checking personal references other than former managers. The reason: No one gives a reference unless he is reasonably certain that kind things will be said about him. The family banker, the local minister, and the friend at the club are poor references at best.

Good reference checking can help to insure a proper fit by identifying the kind of situation and environment in which the applicant performs best. This information can help to avoid a misplacement and, more positively, insure that the job is right for the man and the man is right for the job. Proper reference checking can also yield valuable information about an individual's developmental needs. All this helps to insure retention.

To learn about a candidate's performance on a previous job the investigator has to ascertain what the man did specifically, the circumstances under which he performed, and the results he achieved or failed to achieve. Often this information can be obtained only from the man's manager or from *his* manager.

When the investigator has assembled the performance data he can then determine whether the individual would be doing similar or dissimilar things under the same or different circumstances. Performance standards on the open position could be compared to performance stan-

Exhibit 1-3.
FACTORS IN RETENTION OF EMPLOYEES (A FLOW OF RELEVANT ACTIVITIES IN MANAGING HUMAN ASSETS)

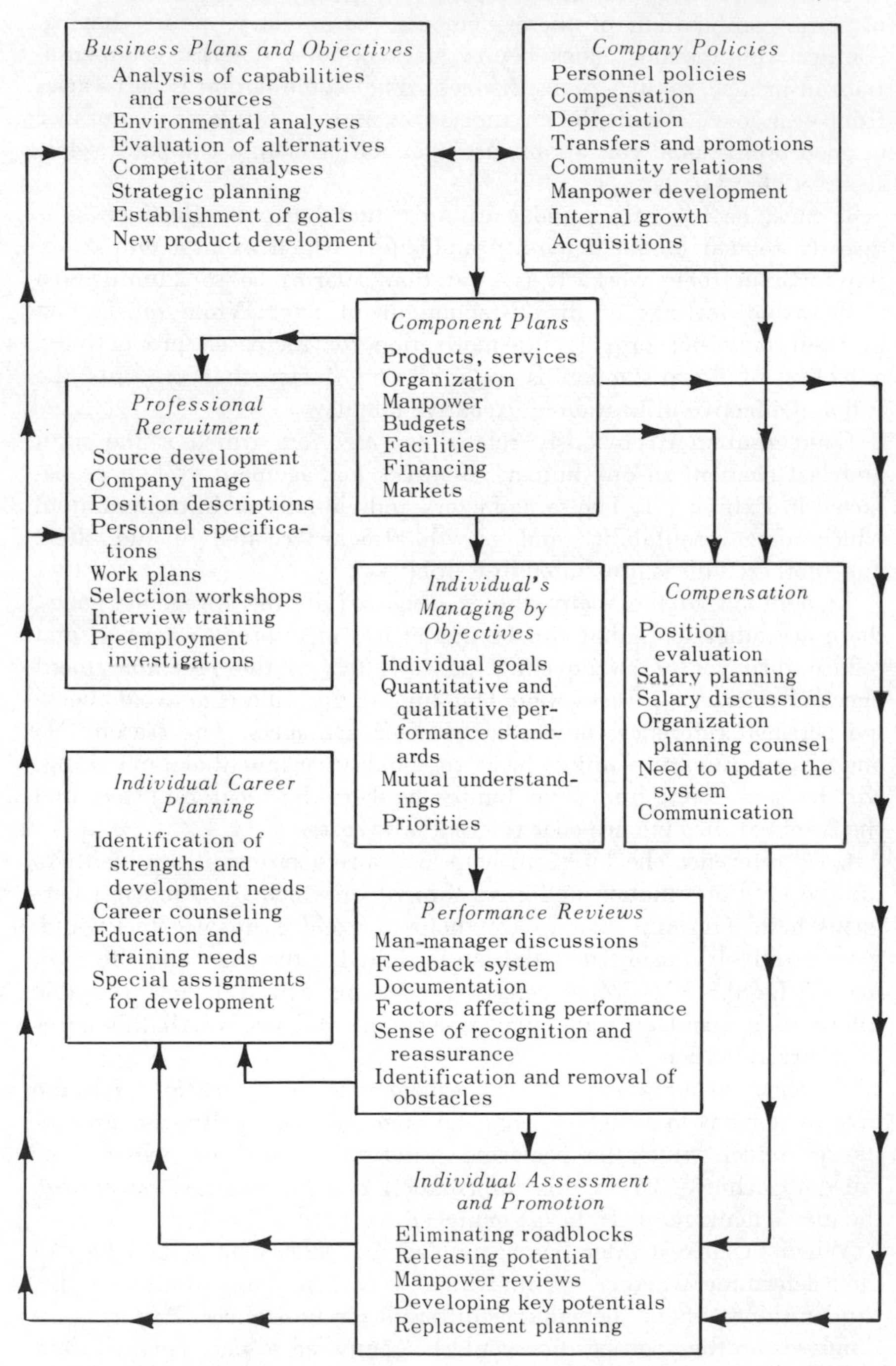

dards on the man's previous position. This gives some real basis for predicting how the man will perform in his new assignment. It is especially relevant to find out what the man did with particular skill as well as to find out where he fell short of his manager's expectations. The standard questions about attendance, dependability, work habits, initiative, strengths, and weaknesses also apply. All these are important factors in retention.

Once the decision has been made to hire a man, orientation, induction, and training appropriate to the position requirements and the man's level of experience and education are essential. The process of industrial socialization must not be left to chance. People need not be left to sink or swim. This is a waste of human assets and almost insures a relatively high turnover rate. The expensive recruiting process must include appropriate induction and orientation.

All too often the common courtesies of industrial socialization are neglected, and the newly hired executive begins his new career treading cautiously until he finds out (somehow) just what he is expected to do and when, and by what standards he is to be measured. Those, too, are essential factors in retention or turnover.

In reality, the entire personnel system from the initial recruitment contact through hiring, orientation, and induction are major factors in retention. They can be as important as having clearly defined goals, priorities, and a sense of timing. Similarly, the attitude survey and the exit interview can prevent people from leaving or at least slow down the flow of voluntary resignations. For key people, a good exit interview can be conducted by the human resources executive. If he has established relationships of mutual trust and confidence, he can learn the real reasons why executives leave. Most have been described already: lack of challenging assignment, oppressive organization climate, limited opportunity for personal and professional growth and development, inadequate compensation, poor organization, lack of communication, and poorly defined responsibilities, goals, and authority. The important thing is to isolate the major reasons for voluntary terminations and then take steps to eliminate the causes. It may even be that a small amount of self-induced turnover will solve a major problem.

Retention, like recruitment, utilization, motivation, compensation, and development, is the result of good management practice. But it must be seen in a new perspective. It is difficult for managers to recognize that they themselves create most of their own problems; it is even more difficult to sell them on the fact that the solution lies with them, through improving their managerial skills and attitudes toward human resource management.

2
The Job of the Human Resources Executive

As a member of top management, the vice-president–human resources must determine what policies, programs, practices, and approaches will contribute most to the realization of the organization's objectives. His position description must take cognizance of the six basic concerns of senior management as described in Chapter 1. This means that in his new role he must be responsible for initiating and implementing—at all levels of management—the most effective utilization of the human assets.

The primary function of the human resources position is to make a major contribution to the development and realization of the organization's short-term and long-range objectives while enabling each employee to develop to the fullest extent of his potential. This requires a catalyst and business effectiveness consultant as contrasted with the traditional role of the personnel director.

With these thoughts in mind, the position of the vice-president–human resources might be defined in this way. He *reports* to the president. His *broad function* is to formulate, recommend, and implement policies, procedures, and plans to insure the most effective planning, recruitment, selection, utilization, motivation, development, and compensation of the organization's human resources; contribute to the development and achievement of the organization's long-range and short-term objectives by initiating and implementing employee relations practices which will enable and encourage each employee to realize his personal goals while maximizing his contribution to business effectiveness; provide for the resolution of management problems and the realization of opportunities through innovative approaches to human resources management.

The *principal responsibilities* of the human resources executive are these.

- Formulate and recommend human resource objectives for inclusion in the organization's overall objectives.

- Identify the potential contribution of good human resource management to organizational objectives.
- Identify management problems that can be resolved and opportunities that can be realized through improved effectiveness in human resource management.
- Formulate, recommend, and implement employee relations policies designed to improve individual productivity, job satisfaction, and profitability.
- Make managers aware of their full responsibilities in the management of the human resources entrusted to them.
- Provide the necessary tools, techniques, and methods which foster the development of a business climate conducive to employee innovation and development.
- Establish the necessary procedures and practices for human resource planning, recruitment, selection, utilization, motivation, development, and compensation. Insure that these are incorporated into every manager's job performance evaluation.
- Develop and staff the employee relations function to make provision for innovative approaches to labor and union relations, personnel practices and services, training and development, communication, community relations, benefit plan development and administration, and problem solving.
- Serve as a catalyst and business effectiveness consultant in initiating and implementing new approaches to human resources management.

This position can exert a tremendous influence on business results. Therefore, a few words need to be said about each principal responsibility.

Just as important as market position, technological leadership, return on investment, and profitability are an organization's human resources. Thus its objectives must reflect this hierarchy of importance.

Human resource objectives for any firm might include five points: (1) Provide stable employment, equitable compensation, desirable working conditions, and opportunities for advancement for employees in return for their skill, care, efforts, dependability, and teamwork. (2) Provide a climate conducive to the development of each employee's potential in accord with his needs, interests, desires, abilities, and willingness to take on additional responsibility to realize his personal and professional career objectives. (3) Manage the human resources to insure continuing vitality and growth of the company while realizing a profit and providing opportunities for public service. (4) Provide a sound organization with enlightened leadership to insure maximum work satisfactions for each employee in a decentralized environment. (5) Define clearly for each individual the responsibilities of his position, along with the commensurate authority that will enable him to make his best contribution to overall organization goals.

Every organization, regardless of its size, must provide for the needs, interests, and desires of its employees within the work environment if it is to earn loyalty, dedication, involvement, and commitment. This is necessary in order to compete effectively for superior talent in the marketplace. Just making these objectives known would serve to attract the kind of employees all organizations want to have. It is, of course, necessary to follow up with good management of human resources, or high turnover will inevitably result.

To shed some light on the importance of human resource management, it is a good exercise to look at the objectives of a profit-oriented enterprise—a single-product company, in this instance—and attempt to identify the potential contribution of effective management of our human assets. The objectives are—

- To obtain and hold 41 percent of the total available market.
- To return 25 percent on invested capital.
- To return 12 percent on sales.
- To be the technological leader in new product innovation.
- To be the leader in introducing new manufacturing processes, methods, and technology.
- To provide a reliable, dependable, safe product at quality levels superior to those of the competition.
- To build public confidence in the company's product and services.
- To attract and retain investor capital by providing a favorable return to shareowners.
- To increase the value of the company's stock.
- To cooperate with and provide a fair profit to our suppliers, distributors, retailers, and contractors.
- To be a good corporate citizen by discharging our social, civic, and economic responsibilities through commitment of funds and managerial talent.

That superior, dedicated people are needed at all levels of the organization to achieve these objectives is evident. The company seeks to maintain a superior position in markets, technology, product, service, quality, and internal and external relationships. In order to do this, all six concerns of top management in obtaining, utilizing, motivating, developing, compensating, and retaining good people must be satisfied. These should be incorporated into the objectives listed above.

For example, in a highly competitive business, even a strong market position cannot be held or improved with mediocre people. It takes the best people, continually giving their best, to attain challenging but achievable goals. It takes people with superior education, training, and experience who are interested in maintaining the initiative in the face of carefully calculated business risks to stay on top of the competitive heap.

It takes people with pride in workmanship who carefully apply their skills and disciplines to produce a marketable product of fine competitive quality on time and within carefully controlled costs. It takes first-line supervisors who are very much aware of the influence they have over their people and who by their example influence them to do their jobs more effectively.

It takes a healthy, profitable company to engage in public service activities. This takes managers with superior skills who recognize and take advantage of opportunities while keeping the wheels turning, the costs down, and the profits up.

It takes broad-gauged managers who see beyond the four walls of their offices to initiate social change and do so profitably, instead of merely reacting to change. It takes managers with special skills in communication, organization, selection, utilization, motivation, and manpower development to make business plans become realities.

In short, the bigger the job to be done, the higher the caliber of person who must be hired to do the job and the more complex and challenging the task of managing him and providing the climate and the environment within which he will put forth his best efforts. Whatever the objective, the human resource is the key factor in its attainment.

Identification and solution of management problems is another responsibility of the human resources executive. As an example, Chapter 3 describes real situations in which management treats the symptoms of underachievement instead of the causes. One of the prerequisites of the human resources executive is to recognize those causes and provide operating management with the tools to reduce the effects or eliminate the conditions that detract from an organization's ability to achieve its goals.

To set guideposts for line management in managing the human asset is a vital part of the human resources executive's responsibility. He does this by formulating and recommending policy for approval by the executive office. Policies are made for several reasons: to insure consistency of action by all managers faced with common decisions; to avoid making the same decisions over and over again; to provide for fair and equitable treatment of all employees in similar situations and circumstances; to communicate top management's major philosophies, values, and attitudes and to translate these into practice; to insure maintenance of a competitive posture in accord with company goals; to communicate top management decisions to all concerned.

Employee relations policies relate to compensation, vacations, holidays, fringe benefits, moving expenses and transfer allowances, performance appraisal, discrimination, termination, severance pay, promotions, manpower development, educational assistance, disciplinary action and discharge, and communication. There are others, but these are among the most relevant for a progressive organization. Examples are included in the Appendix.

Good, sound, up-to-date employee relations policies, well administered, help to prevent conflict and internal dissension. They clarify and communicate. They provide guidelines for managerial decisions on human resource questions. They help to recruit high-caliber executives. As an example, if a company's compensation policy provides for payment above the going rate for executive talent, the recruiting job is made immeasurably easier. Money is important, particularly at the middle management levels. Add to the dollars a sound fringe benefit package, including a holiday and vacation schedule on the liberal side for the industry, and chances of winning over a prospect are further enhanced. Couple this with a formal policy of education assistance, including a plan for the individual's career development, and the chances are enhanced even further. As the candidate sees his job responsibility spelled out, visualizes how and where he can contribute, perceives his avenues for advancement, and then finds it will cost him nothing to relocate his family, the odds heavily favor the company in the recruitment market.

Let's face it: Some managers are naturally generous; some are naturally tight-fisted. While both may have a strong sense of stewardship, policy guidelines generate much better employee relations by providing for relatively equal treatment of job candidates and employees already on the payroll. They reduce the number of managerial headaches.

Most managers eventually become aware that their skills as individual contributors are not the major ingredients for success as managers. They soon acquire, through schooling and experience, the rudiments of planning, organizing, controlling, and measuring. But all too often they concentrate these managerial skills on physical and material resources while neglecting the fact that people needs must be planned for just as meticulously as maintenance needs for conveyor systems.

It is a major responsibility of the human resources executive to make all managers fully aware of their stewardship and accountability for the human resources entrusted to their care. Organization and manpower planning, control, and measurement are the real causes of managerial success or failure. Managerial attitudes can be changed. Such

Exhibit 2-1.
HUMAN RESOURCES FUNCTIONAL ORGANIZATION CHART

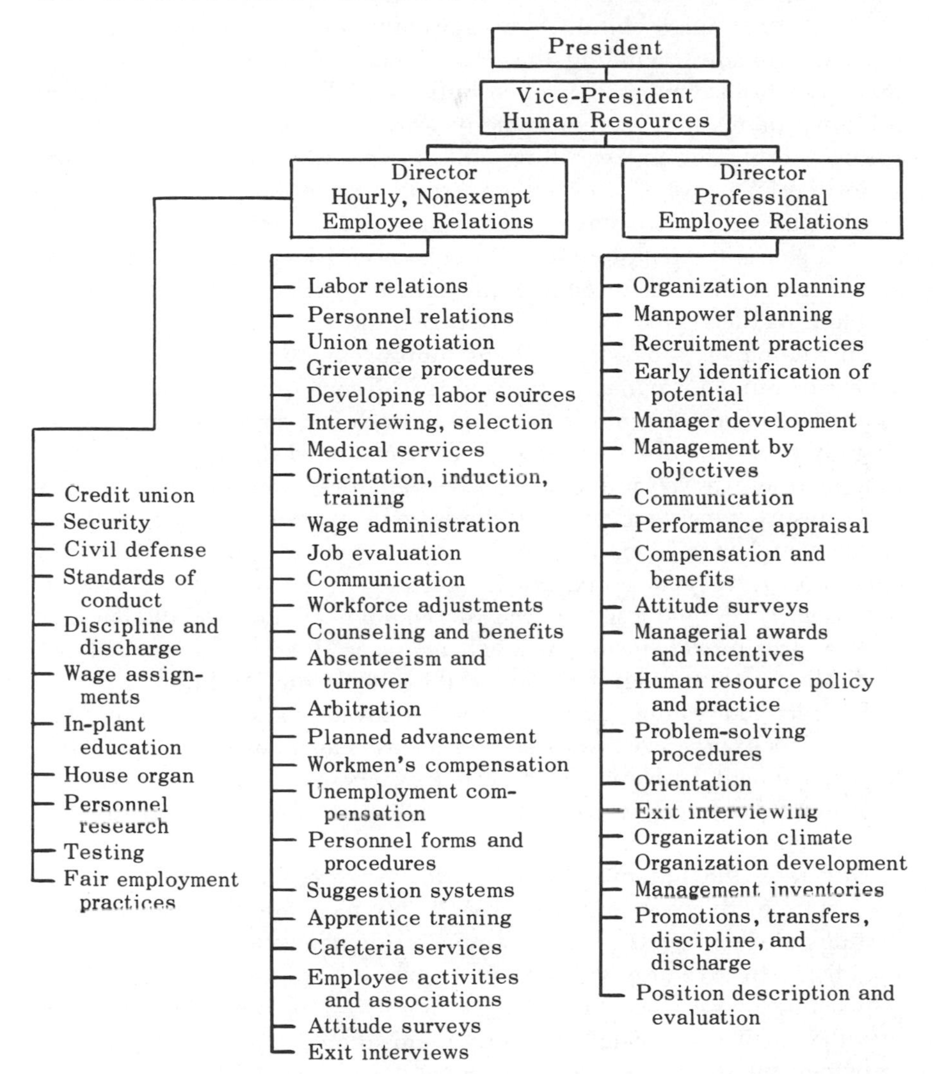

change begins with an awareness of the vast importance of the human asset, then must come an understanding of needs for new skills, and, finally, acceptance and implementation of sound human relations policies, practices, and procedures. This does not happen overnight, but constant attention and education can bring about favorable change.

In addition to making all managers aware of their stewardship responsibility for human resources, the human resources executive must go farther and provide the *training*, along with simple, workable procedures—the *tools* and *techniques* to assist managers in discharging this responsibility.

These procedures should cover virtually every people concern of top management, including the development of an organizational climate which encourages employee initiative. They range from a determination of manpower requirements—an analysis of the present and future workforce—to recruiting and interviewing techniques, counseling, performance appraisal, goal setting, attitude surveys, and control of absenteeism and turnover. They incorporate organization planning as well as manpower planning through careful identification of future experience requirements stated in concise position descriptions.

They include provision for action ranging from soliciting and processing employee suggestions to cost improvements to sales and supervisory training to manager development. Techniques to assist in employee selection, communication, discipline, and performance review should be part of every manager's book of knowledge and skills. The human resources executive must make all these, and more, available.

To insure consistency and uniformity in applying human resource fundamentals, the human resources executive must also *establish workable procedures and practices.* He must personally insure that each manager learns and uses all the aforementioned tools in discharging his stewardship responsibility. Each manager should be measured periodically on how well he applies these tools and techniques.

In order to accomplish all this, the employee relations function must be developed, organized, and staffed to provide innovative approaches to management problems. A typical functional organization chart for a medium- to large-size company is shown in Exhibit 2-1. Only the key functions are listed.

In effect, the human resources executive becomes a catalyst and business effectiveness consultant. With his focus on the management of human resources, he must convince all managers, starting at the top, that effective use of human resources is a series of disciplines which must be learned and can be taught. He becomes the salesman and the teacher. No longer can an organization merely react and contribute to the misuse of human assets.

3
Selecting the Human Resources Executive

What kind of man does it take to successfully discharge the responsibilities outlined in the preceding chapter?

The very first requirement is to think like a profit-oriented line executive. This kind of thought process necessitates an understanding of what is involved in operating a decentralized business, including customer acceptance of its products and the achievement of profitable results commensurate with business risks.

To be a successful human resources executive takes a realization of what a complex process it is to research, design, produce, and market a competitive quality product. It takes professional training in how to provide good jobs, equitable compensation, pleasant work environment, job satisfactions, stable employment, and planned avenues of career advancement. It requires the ability to teach and inspire others to manage both human and material resources for sustained, healthy, profitable growth and public service. This is necessary to attract and retain investor capital.

The job necessitates know-how in obtaining voluntary action to meet a company's obligations and responsibilities in civic life as a good corporate citizen and to maintain a high degree of cooperation with suppliers, dealers, and distributors who help to facilitate production, distribution, sale, and service of a company's products.

The task is to identify and place into proper priority order the human relations opportunities to contribute to the success of the business. This means persuading managers to relate good employee relations practice to the improvement of current performance and in the process improve their leadership skills. This implies a job marketing concept. In other words, just as good product + effective selling = customer acceptance, so a good job + effective selling = employee acceptance. It is the manager who, by his own actions, earns employee acceptance, understanding, and cooperation. A good human resources executive knows from experience that people tend to accept improvements as a matter of course, and if their expectations are not realistic, they tend to be disappointed and even resentful.

Focus on Productivity and Profitability

The human resources executive must know the business; he must view it from a wide variety of perspectives. He must put himself in the place of the top management team and constantly bear in mind the pressures for reduced costs, improved profits, increased market share, and so on that occupy the thoughts and hence command the top priorities of the president and the senior executives in marketing, manufacturing, finance and controls, engineering, and administration. Since these executives must become numbers-oriented, any real gains in human asset management will be made by way of the numbers approach. This is entirely reasonable, and a practical human resources executive seeks his opportunities accordingly in those areas of greatest potential impact on profits. Failure to recognize this relegates the employee relations function to a clerical function—excluded from participation in top management decisions and policy considerations.

The human resources executive must become involved in the business through learning its niche in the marketplace; its competitive advantages and disadvantages; its future direction; its changing technology; its growth rate; its distribution patterns; its breakeven point; its cyclical variations, if any; the factors most pertinent for success in each functional discipline; and the real problems and opportunities at the top of the organization as well as in the shop. Then he can begin to relate his skills to the practical solution of very real problems and the pursuit of growth opportunities with appropriate calculated, balanced risks.

It is the human resources executive who must comprehend, translate, convince top executives of the importance of, and implement a *balanced-best-interest concept*. This concept recognizes that there are no less than five groups of contributor–claimants who make a distinct and recognizable contribution to the success of the business and who, by virtue of this contribution, have a claim on its assets. They are all human resources of the business. These are the five groups.

Employees. We must provide them with the job satisfactions described in Chapter 1 or we will not be able to recruit or retain them, let alone provide the climate that will make them want to contribute their best efforts and loyalty or give us their understanding, appreciation, cooperation, and support.

Shareowners. A company's owners look for a good return on their investment, a good steady growth rate for appreciation, and the quality of stewardship responsibility that they have entrusted to their team of professional managers. If these are lacking, below par, or unsatisfactory, the owners can withdraw their capital, file suits, and eventually replace management.

Customers. Nowadays customers demand competitive quality, service, price, reliability, durability, performance, and reputation. The firm that meets these needs, that recognizes and provides esthetic values, will survive and grow and prosper. A firm that ignores or fails to recognize these very real considerations will lose its customers and will eventually go broke.

The public at large and the plant community. This is the area of corporate citizenship. We are now in an era of concern for the welfare of people and society and the ecology. Social and economic problems demand the attention of business. At stake is the ability to attract top people and win community support, community cooperation. These are the times for close and continuous cooperation of management, labor, government, and education to solve the pressing problems of society. No company, regardless of size, can ignore these relationships beyond its four walls. To do so is to court disaster. The progressive firm looks to the resolution of social and environmental problems as opportunities and finds creative ways to solve the problems while at the same time realizing an appropriate return on its investment of managerial time, materials, and money.

Governments—federal, state, and local. These relationships are closely akin to those described with regard to the public at large. Business must insure that its tax dollars get the best mileage possible. This implies responsible, mature government. Education, housing, zoning, utilities, industrial development, courts, fire and police protection, ordinances, and laws are all tied together in government relations. The consequences of ignoring this vital group of contributor-claimants are obvious. It is a form of enlightened self-interest to insure mature, responsible government.

The human resources executive recognizes that management must pay heed to this balanced-best-interest concept. In part, this means that he cannot "rob Peter to pay Paul." It means that wage and salary costs must be viewed in light of their effects on the other four groups of contributor-claimants. Similarly, increasing a dividend payout or lowering prices to the customer cannot be financed out of employee paychecks or by pounding on suppliers. The point is that effective human resource management has broad implications. These must be dealt with and given proper consideration in the full spectrum of human relationships.

Similarly, an in-depth understanding of employee needs as spelled out in Chapter 1 has to be translated into everyday management practice. It must stand side by side, complementary to and compatible with the constant need for productivity and profitability improvement.

Identifying Real Problems and Opportunities

By now it is apparent that human resource management involves a good leader, a healthy work environment, and a good job to produce a motivated employee. A results-oriented approach to employee relations requires management skills in identifying problems, setting priorities, and developing and evaluating alternatives as well as the ability to communicate, initiate action, implement it, measure it, control it, and change its course as necessary.

The roots of most management problems lie in the organization's misuse of its human resources. In most cases this is not deliberate, but is a problem of inattention resulting from a lack of knowledge of how to identify the real causes of those problems.

In Exhibit 3-1 we see the causes, effects, and proposed solutions to employee dissatisfactions. These problems cannot be resolved by taking stringent punitive measures, by adding inspectors, by threats, or by spending more money. The human resources executive is well aware that the real causes are poor human relations practices at all levels of management. Any of the problem areas may be a result or manifestation of any one or several of the listed causes. Good managers do not treat the symptoms; they root out the underlying causes. The human resources executive assists in the process and, in large measure, provides the solutions. The end result is a permanent and lasting cure and hence reduced costs and increased productivity.

Effective human relations does not happen by chance; it is the result of careful management planning, implementation, and follow-up. Professional training is a prerequisite. Therefore, a number of professional disciplines are stressed in the following specification for the human resources executive.

Personnel Specifications for Human Resources Executive

Age. Over 30; it is highly doubtful if anyone under 30 years of age could have acquired the skills included in this personnel specification.

Exhibit 3-1.
POOR HUMAN ASSET UTILIZATION: CAUSES, EFFECTS, AND SUGGESTED SOLUTIONS

TYPICAL PROBLEM AREAS	REAL CAUSES	SOLUTIONS
Low productivity	No goals or poorly defined goals	Management by objectives
High turnover and absenteeism	Inadequate or ineffective communication	Predetermined performance standards
High recruiting costs	Untrained supervision	Appraisal system and follow-up
Poor product quality	Poor orientation, induction procedures	Competitive compensation system, well administered
Excessive scrap	Autocratic or dictatorial management styles	Attitudinal training
Failure to meet schedules	Inadequate training or no training at all	Sensitivity training; organization development
Lack of new ideas on product, process, distribution, sales	Inattention to employee dissatisfactions	Early identification program
Lack of depth in the organization	Lack of employee participation and involvement	Organization planning
Failure to meet sales objectives	Lack of commitment, sense of urgency	Frequent, open labor-management meetings
Labor problems	Inadequate personnel to do the job	Formal grievance procedures
Clogging of paperwork pipelines		Management development
High accident rates		Planned advancement
Wildcat strikes		Attitude surveys
The underachieving capital project		Exit interviews
Loss of market share		Selection workshops
Exceeding budgets and poor returns on investment		Clear statements of policies, procedures, and rules
		Communication at all levels
		Clear identification of responsibilities, priorities, authority, and accountability

Education. Minimum of a bachelor's degree, preferably in psychology, the behavioral sciences, communication, or business administration. If possible, a master's degree in business administration, the behavioral sciences, or psychology.

Knowledge. Modern management tools and techniques such as organization, information systems, accounting and finance; business planning; controls; personnel management tools and techniques, including job evaluation, compensation, manpower planning, union relations, training and development; understanding of motivation, utilization, and recruitment tools, techniques, and practices.

Experience. At least 15 years of progressively more responsible, successful assignments as specialist, supervisor, and manager in a manufacturing enterprise, including:

- Organization planning and manpower planning.
- Management by objectives.
- Supervisory and manager development.
- Communication.
- Performance appraisal systems.
- Personnel and union relations.
- Recruitment (including executive search).
- Compensation and benefits.
- Policy formulation and administration.
- Behavioral sciences, applied.
- Manpower inventories.
- Workforce adjustments.
- Orientation, induction, and training.
- Preparation of position descriptions and job evaluations and establishment of performance standards.
- Personnel practices: cafeteria, safety, testing, research, fair employment, attitude surveys, workmen's compensation, unemployment compensation, suggestion systems, security.

Demonstrated skills and abilities. These must include the following:

- Ability to identify and resolve real management problems.
- Ability to work with senior management, line and staff.
- Interviewing skills in employment, discipline and discharge, promotion, transfer, layoff, orientation, exit interviewing.
- Counseling.
- Ability to speak and write clearly, concisely, and effectively.
- Motivation.
- Leadership, as demonstrated by the ability to build an effective team.
- Ability to identify and implement innovative approaches to the solution of employee relations problems.
- Planning, organizing, integrating, controlling, and measuring.
- Decision making, as to both quality and timing.
- Teaching.
- Priorities.
- Negotiating.

Personal characteristics. These must include the following:

- Flexibility and adaptability.
- High energy level coupled with good health.

- Dynamic leadership ability.
- Creativity; willingness to try new approaches and take calculated risks.
- Results orientation, with a need to achieve.
- Service orientation.
- Sensitivity and concern for others.
- Ability to relate with equal effectiveness to top managers as well as hourly rated employees.

4
Formulating Human Resource Objectives

In previous chapters, the job of the human resources executive was defined in relation to management concerns, needs, problems, and opportunities. It is now time to consider the variety of situations that must be taken into account in the formulation of employee relations objectives. Any objective must recognize the character of the workforce and clearly identify its real needs so as to prepare management for the problems and opportunities that lie ahead in human resource management.

The human resources executive of tomorrow will be responsible for a bimodal workforce. In other words, a greater proportion of the workforce than ever before will be concentrated at the two extremes. The top 15 percent will be composed of professional and managerial employees and the bottom 15 percent will come from the ranks of the disadvantaged. Because these two groups will make up so big a segment of the workforce, their problems will be the focus of increasing attention as their impact is felt throughout the organization.

The top 15 percent are demanding more freedom, more latitude in decision making, and more say-so in the selection and execution of work assignments as well as the standards by which their performance will be measured. Soon, opportunities for continuing education and self-development will be part of the job offer. They will pay more attention to career planning and clearly defined avenues of advancement. They are programmed for lifelong learning.

The bottom 15 percent represent the poorly educated urban population. These are the ghetto dwellers—people with little motivation who have lived in poverty and have been deprived of job opportunities, experience, and education for many years. Understanding the viewpoint, attitudes, and posture of these new entrants into the workforce may be necessary for survival for many organizations.

Faced with these polar opposites—each requiring different skills and abilities—the human resources executive must formulate balanced objectives based on the needs, problems, and opportunities in his particular situation. The objectives presented in this chapter reflect this balanced concern. Although the representative objectives described for a single-product company in Chapter 2 could be applicable anywhere, regardless of location, the supportive human resource objectives must take full cognizance of a specific situation—the community business climate, labor supply and demand, types of employees available, the present status of human asset management, and the state of affairs in employee selection, utilization, motivation, development, compensation, and retention.

Let us assume that an employee relations audit has been made—through an attitude survey (as described later in this chapter), exit interviews, analysis of pertinent statistics and problem areas, and so on—and that the following composite balanced human resource objectives have been established:

1. Reduce employee turnover from 57 percent to 37 percent per year.
2. Develop and install an hourly job evaluation program.
3. Overhaul the exempt salaried compensation program.
4. Review, audit, and improve employee services.
5. Establish a system for early identification of managerial potential.
6. Initiate and implement a new approach to manager development.
7. Improve communication with employees.
8. Develop and implement a maintenance training program.
9. Develop and implement a new system for making rapid workforce adjustments up and down.

For each of the foregoing objectives, let us consider the background situation which led to its formulation, the action steps leading to its fulfillment, and, where possible, the anticipated results. The various responsibilities along with key relationships and starting and completion dates need not concern us here.

The first objective is to *reduce employee turnover from 57 percent to 37 percent per year*. Within the past two years employee turnover has risen from 37 to 57 percent per year. Industry has grown rapidly in the area, and unemployment has dropped from 6 percent to 1.5 percent. It has become necessary to lower recruitment standards in order to hire sufficient numbers of people to maintain a two-shift operation. There has been no formal orientation, induction, or training program in the past. The plant employs 800 people. Cost of turnover per employee is estimated to be $600. A number of studies have been made of the cost of hourly employee turnover, and the cost per employee ranges from $500 to $12,000. This includes identifiable scrap, rework, lost-time accidents, doctor visits, direct recruiting costs, clerical costs, training time, and loss of productivity during the training period before average proficiency is reached. For this objective, nine action steps are indicated.

1. Develop new labor sources and more fully utilize present labor sources to attract a higher caliber of employees; for example, local high schools, state employment offices, local church groups, young people's organizations, YMCA. Set up satellite recruiting offices; work with civic, social, welfare, and fraternal organizations and trade and vocational schools to promote company image, reputation, job opportunities; and wage and benefits package.
2. Implement new formal orientation, induction, training, and follow-up procedures. Involve all personnel who meet and work with new employees, including plant security personnel, medical services staff, employment clerks and interviewers, foremen, union representatives, and appropriate long-service employees who will assist in training new employees.
3. Work with industrial engineering in reviewing typical employment entry jobs to attempt to make them more interesting and varied wherever possible; to reduce training time and increase chances of early success; to remove or ameliorate disagreeable conditions where possible, and otherwise to humanize the work. Where necessary, modify standards for new employees during the training period.
4. Review—and, where appropriate, revise—pay rates, number of transfers of new employees, progression rates. Make promotional and transfer opportunities more readily available as jobs open up throughout the operation.
5. Assign senior employees as counselors to assist new employees in calculating their pay, securing locker assignments, resolving problems and difficulties, and improving any unsatisfactory conditions.
6. Hold special first-line supervisory training sessions to emphasize the need for fair, consistent, and humane treatment of new employees. Stress precise and frequent communication coupled with patience and listening skills. Measure first-line supervisors on turnover improvement.
7. Analyze turnover in terms of age, sex, marital status, citizenship, geographic location, and other demographic factors, as well as department, unit, length of time on the job, foreman, job, and shift. Detect patterns, if any, and move in with appropriate corrective action as necessary.
8. Develop a system of incentives for length of service with appropriate bonuses at regular intervals.
9. Conduct regular follow-up meetings with new employees to learn their needs and to ask for their evaluation of orientation and attitudinal training. Stress in-plant education.

Achievement of this goal would represent a cost saving of $96,000 per year. The figure is arrived at in this way: The present average annual turnover is 456 employees (800 employees × 57 percent per year). The target is a turnover of 296 employees (800 employees × 37 percent per year). The reduction of 160 (456 — 296) multiplied by the cost for each case of turnover ($600) equals an annual cost improvement of $96,000.

The second objective is to *develop and install an hourly job evaluation program.* There has been no formal job evaluation in the past, nor have any outside surveys been made for wage comparison purposes. Hourly wage base rates are established by past practice and individual negotiation. Job descriptions are nonexistent, and there is valid reason to believe that duplication of effort and undesirable overlap are occurring daily. Because of the apparent inequity in wage rates, the longer-service employees with the highest degree of skills are underutilized. This is true because there is not a sufficient wage differential to make more complex jobs attractive to experienced employees. Conversely, too many dollars are being paid for jobs with low skill requirements. The net result is that some employees are overpaid while others are underpaid. New employees are assigned work that is too difficult and exacting, thus contributing to a high scrap rate, reduced quality, and low productivity. Avenues for advancement are clearly absent, and training of new employees is haphazard because the whole job is never really spelled out. For this objective, eight *action steps* are indicated.

1. Prepare individual job descriptions for each clearly identifiable and distinctly different full-time job. Have both supervisor and employee fill in questionnaires about each job, supplement with personal interviews as needed.
2. Classify all clearly defined jobs by job families and/or by skill requirement—for example, fabrication, machinery, assembly, finishing, packaging, shipping, materials handling, supportive. Possibly also classify into highly skilled, skilled, semiskilled, or unskilled.
3. Develop an appropriate job evaluation manual tailored to the company's needs. Stress a weighted point system for objectivity and precision in measuring such factors as education, experience, skills, effort, and working conditions. Be sure to evaluate the requirements of the job, *not* the qualifications of the person assigned to that job.
4. Conduct local wage surveys with comparable firms in the area, using common bench mark jobs to check the accuracy of the point evaluation and to establish the basis for a wage structure.
5. Establish an appropriate wage structure with a sufficient number of wage rates and rate ranges to allow for wage growth with increasing

proficiency on the same job and to provide significant pay increases for promotional opportunities.

6. Implement the new wage plan according to a predetermined time schedule. Correct inequities such as overpayments and underpayments as circumstances permit. Develop wage administration guidelines to insure fair, equitable, uniform, and consistent treatment throughout the organization.

7. Conduct periodic audits and follow-up. The best system requires semiannual maintenance and review and appraisal.

8. Communicate the new approach to all employees before the start of the program and before, during, and after each phase.

If this objective is properly implemented, the following five results should occur:

1. Elimination of 10 hourly rated jobs because of duplication: 10 × $6,000 per year each = $60,000 cost improvement.
2. Reduced scrap rate for new employees, who will be assigned to new entry jobs requiring lesser skills.
3. Improved ability to fill more demanding and exacting jobs because there will be sufficient wage incentive for more highly skilled, longer-service employees to want those jobs.
4. Improved productivity in first few weeks of employment because of provision for systematic training and because requirements will be clearly spelled out through the job description.
5. Overall lower total wage costs because premium rates will no longer be paid for unskilled and semiskilled work.

The third objective is to *overhaul the exempt salaried compensation program*. Attitude surveys and exit interviews strongly indicate that two out of three voluntary resignations of exempt, salaried employees are due in large measure to feelings of dissatisfaction associated with compensation. Specifically, employees note that there has been no upgrading of the exempt salaried pay structure for the past five years; individual pay increases have failed to keep pace with increases in the cost of living; pay increases are granted every 16 months on the average, and there seems to be a tendency to give uniform pay increases, thus failing to recognize superior performance while overpaying mediocre and poor performers. A significant contributing factor here is the absence of position descriptions, performance standards, and performance appraisals. Also contributing to the problem is an absence of control on the number of people hired by certain functions, and formal organization planning is nonexistent. Ten *action steps* are indicated for this objective.

1. Make a thorough analysis of the existing compensation system and pay practices to ascertain the magnitude of the problem.
2. Develop a position description for each position, working with the incumbent and his manager.
3. Classify and evaluate each position in relation to other positions within the same function and in relation to comparable positions inside and outside the company.
4. Establish an appropriate salary structure with rate ranges for each grade within the structure. Use comparative industry salary data so as to keep rates competitive.
5. Identify out-of-line actual pay rates—on the low side as well as the high side. Program for corrective action in both cases.
6. Establish salary administration policy and issue guidelines; maintain and update these every six months.
7. Communicate before, during, and after each of the foregoing steps.
8. Concurrent with the foregoing steps, work with all managers to insure the establishment of performance standards and priorities for each exempt salaried position. Such standards should be set with the participation of incumbents whose performance will be evaluated on the basis of those standards.
9. Develop and implement a formal performance appraisal system; at least once a year, each person should have his performance reviewed with him by his manager.
10. Consider individual salary adjustments at least once every 12 months, and relate such adjustments to demonstrated accomplishment and improved job performance as measured against predetermined standards.

Implementation of this approach should result in reduced salary costs and improved productivity. It will make the exempt recruitment job easier because there will be fewer candidates to hire, given reduced turnover. Spelling out the requirements for each job means that more well-qualified people will be hired because of a better fit. Over a period of time, fewer people will be needed because clearly defined position responsibilities coupled with effective organization and manpower planning will help to eliminate duplication of effort, defensive maneuvering, and empire building. Each position will have to justify its existence by showing a direct contribution to the achievement of organizational objectives—otherwise, it should be eliminated. If a position cannot be described in these terms, in all likelihood it is a luxury the organization can ill afford.

The fourth objective is to *review, audit, and improve employee services*. Each year the company spends in excess of $50,000 for employee activities: picnics, Christmas parties, service awards, and the like. The company subsidizes the lunch program. Total costs of these fringe benefits approximate 18 percent of actual payroll costs. The personnel function grew without appropriate direction or control; a number of existing programs were inherited and many new ones were initiated. Employee surveys indicate dissatisfaction with the food services, the recreation program, the benefit plans, the suggestion system, the service awards program, and the company's paternalistic attitude. Managers have confirmed that administration of these areas has left a great deal to be desired, and a few seem to benefit at the expense of the many. For this objective, seven *action steps* are indicated.

1. After investigating all complaints, determine where the best mileage can be obtained by the company for the many dollars invested in employee activities and services.

2. Reallocate available funds to those areas which have proved to be of most value to the employees and to the company.

3. Gradually reduce company subsidies to the credit union, the recreation association, the canteen fund, and the numerous other organizations and special events.

4. Set up strict measures of accountability for all funds received from vended services. Control the use and disbursement of these funds.

5. Communicate to employees that these actions are a response to their expressed dissatisfactions. In all cases, where fewer activities or organizations or lesser benefits result, superior administration and the benefit of the many rather than the few will have to be given priority. If employees have to be coaxed to support an activity, chances are that it is not worth the expenditure to bolster and support it.

6. Treat all benefit costs as business expenses and measure the return wherever possible. If the benefit has a favorable impact on employee support, loyalty, and understanding, consider its continuance, but run and control it properly. If it has a negative impact on attitudes, productivity, costs, or profits, correct the deficiencies or abandon the activity.

7. Frequently communicate and show by example the company's intentions to provide good jobs and benefits fully comparable with other concerns that compete in the same labor market. Make it clear that excessive fringe benefit costs do not bring about proportionate benefits to shareowners or employees.

By being competitive in fringe benefit costs, over a three-year period the company can reduce its actual outlay of dollars from 18 to 16 percent of total payroll costs. This estimate is based on surveys of what comparable firms are doing for their employees. The object is to get the dollars to work as hard as the people do while providing greater satisfactions than in the past and at the same time minimizing dissatisfactions.

The fifth objective is to *establish a system for early identification of managerial potential.* A recent review of all managerial performance ratings and evaluation of near-term promotables determined that no backup candidates will be available for at least the next three years for 46 of the 58 key management positions. There is an annual rating form in existence, but it is not quantitative and measures social characteristics as opposed to tangible accomplishment. The form is not discussed with the employee and is used only as part of the overall salary review. The company is growing in sales volume at the rate of 10 percent per year. An age analysis of the managerial group indicates that 38 of the 58 key people can be expected to retire, die, resign, or be relocated within the next five years. Couple this with the projected need for a 10 percent increase in all managerial positions to take advantage of growth opportunities, and it is obvious that immediate attention must be directed toward early identification of young hopefuls who have high potential. Six *action steps* are indicated for this objective.

1. Use the performance appraisal system which will be developed in conjunction with the third objective—an overhaul of the exempt compensation plan—to identify salaried employees between the ages of 25 and 35 who show promise for accelerated growth and development.

2. Interview the immediate manager of each individual identified to determine the degree to which each possesses the following attributes:

- Ability to master new assignments quickly.
- Ability to obtain cooperation and assistance from those not responsible to him.
- Initiative in assuming additional responsibilities.
- Aggressiveness and decisiveness, but without lessened sensitivity to people.
- Communication skills—oral and written; skill in listening as well as speaking and writing.

3. Request the managers of those identified to obtain the concurrence of *their* managers since they will also be involved in the selection, development, and promotion decisions. Each manager of a high-potential nominee should then interview his nominee to ascertain:

- Interest in and desire for advancement.
- Any limitations: geographic, health, attitude, and so on.

- Willingness to make personal sacrifices for advancement: acceptance of additional developmental assignments; related night school studies; long hours and constant pressure.
- Personal and professional goals and timetable, if any.

The human resources executive or an outside consultant will have to train managers to conduct these interviews or actually conduct the interviews himself.

4. Each year the group identified should be carefully appraised and anyone who fails to measure up should be culled out. At the same time, new candidates who have merited consideration through superior performance should be added.

5. Manpower inventories should be established containing such information as an individual's age, appraisals, rating of potential, experience, education, salary history, strengths, limitations, needs, and interests. A good retrieval system should be established as part of the inventory system.

6. Organization planning and replacement charts should be constructed, highlighting areas of immediate, near-term, and long-term needs. These will suggest the kinds of education and experience to go into an individual's development plan.

Having completed these steps, the company is now ready for a formal manager development effort. While it is difficult to place a dollar value on an early identification effort, such an effort provides a sound basis for manager development. This means having good people available to fill key positions and avoiding the costly mistakes of bad promotion decisions.

The sixth objective is to *initiate and implement a new approach to manager development*. This is obviously related to the preceding objective, and the same situation therefore prevails. It is recognized by senior management that manager development is essential for corporate survival and growth. It is one of the most important ingredients for technological leadership in methods, processes, and products. The presence or absence of manager development greatly influences employee morale and attitude. It reflects and represents the company's concern for the advancement of its employees. It significantly influences the company's ability to compete in the marketplace. It is essential for the realization of short- and long-term objectives.

It will therefore be the policy of the company to prepare individuals for promotion well in advance of actual job openings—a thing that has not been done in the past. This new policy of promotion from within is formulated to do three things: (1) provide a continuing supply of competent, well-trained supervisory and managerial personnel to meet company needs for executive talent; (2) assist each exempt salaried employee to realize his maximum potential; (3) provide opportunities for all exempt employees to maintain and update skills and abilities required for superior performance. Nine *action steps* are indicated for this objective.

1. Each manager, starting with the president, should review the three- to five-year business plan for his operation including changes in markets, products, technology, information requirements, economics, and political and social conditions. He should then evolve an organization structure, working in conjunction with his key people, which seems to best meet the identified, anticipated future changes.

2. Each manager should then note the specific new requirements for each future position in terms of knowledge, skills, attitudes, experience, and abilities.

3. Having already identified his strongest and poorest performers by means of the new performance appraisal system, the manager should construct an organization replacement chart—identifying possible candidates for future positions and indicating their state of readiness.

4. Each candidate's dossier should be completed as part of a central manager manpower inventory.

5. The manager should then assess present and future requirements against availability of requisite human resources.

6. Having already identified voids and gaps as they relate to individual needs (including the people in the early identification program), the manager, in conjunction with the human resources executive, should develop individual career plans tailored to the needs of the operation while giving full cognizance to individual needs, interests, and abilities.

7. Career plans will necessitate in-house education and experience as well as supplemented outside individual and group training. There will often be areas of common need, and in these cases group classes could be highly beneficial. Such classes might include cost control and financial management analysis; managerial skills in planning, organizing, control, and measurement of physical, material, financial, and human resources; communication; managerial economics; and marketing.

Individual voids and gaps can be filled through a time-phased, accelerated sequence of events which might include task force assignments; job enlargement; "assistant to" assignments; job rotation; promotional and lateral transfers; geographic relocation; multiplant, product, and industry exposure; and multifunctional exposure. At each phase and at each step, progress should be carefully recorded and measured to insure that the right candidates have been chosen for manager development.

8. Management by objectives should be initiated at the senior management level in order to (a) provide on-the-job training and development through accomplishment of goals, priorities, and timetables agreed upon by each man and his manager; (b) permit and encourage individual opportunity for success; (c) improve present job performance; (d) produce the environment in which the job is shaped and controlled by the man in close working relationship with his manager; (e) provide a meaningful tool that will objectively evaluate performance and act as an early warning system to detect deviations from plan so that adjustments and revisions can be made.

9. All of the foregoing must be directly related to the revised compensation plan and to the early identification program.

The result should show a significant improvement in current business operations in all areas where performance targets were established by the man. Individual commitment and involvement produce the best results. Experience has shown that individual and group productivity significantly improve while fostering the development process.

The seventh objective is to *improve communication with employees.* Within the past few years, the company has grown rapidly as industry demand exceeded all expectations. Market share, however, has fallen off; quality and productivity consistently fail to meet standards; absenteeism has become a problem; and generally employees do not appear to be responsive to the needs of the business. There is no house organ, nor are any formal meetings held with the exception of the monthly executive staff policy committee. Management has become aware of the need to improve communication.

Teamwork is a prerequisite for success in any business venture, including the introduction of new products, methods, procedures, and systems. To have teamwork, there must be mutual respect and loyalty between employer and employee. The employee who is convinced of the good intentions of management is inclined to accept the validity of what management says.

It is the policy of the company to encourage and promote frank and continuing communication on all matters which affect employees' jobs and welfare and to provide the programs, methods, and media to implement this policy at all levels in the organization.

An improvement in communication should help to enlist full employee cooperation and support of management goals, objectives, and programs. This can be accomplished to the degree that employees understanding, accept, and appreciate their jobs, their benefits, and management's good intentions. Management should attempt to acquaint employees with the problems and opportunities facing the company. Advance communications should be designed to prevent rumors and the spread of misinformation. There is room for everyone—top and bottom—to learn to listen and understand and appreciate the other person's viewpoint. Communication will not substitute for "doing right voluntarily" in human relations matters, however. Management credibility must be earned through demonstrated results. Eight *action steps* are indicated for this objective.

1. Administer attitude surveys to determine the present level and quality of communication and management action in such areas as job satisfaction, quality of supervision, operating efficiency, compensation, group harmony, future opportunity, general management, orientation, performance appraisal, work planning, and working conditions. Plan a follow-up survey in two years to measure the degree of improvement—if any. Have an outside service tabulate the results and prepare the reports.

2. Communicate attitude survey results, especially to those who can effect improvements. Set specific measurable improvement goals and follow up on them.

3. Schedule semiannual business report meetings to be conducted by the chief executive and his staff for all employees. The subject matter can be broad and specific, and it should stress problems, opportunities, new products, expectations, business climate, corporate community relations, goals, and objectives.

4. Each manager should hold one staff meeting with his people each week to exchange pertinent information. Minutes of this meeting should be forwarded to the manager's manager.

5. Supervisory development meetings should be held by the human resources executive for first-line supervisors and their managers once a week. Pertinent human resource considerations should determine the agenda for each meeting.

6. Each supervisor should meet with all his employees in small groups at least once a month to share experiences, solve problems, and make general improvements.

7. The approaches to orientation, induction, training, performance appraisal, and exit interviewing should be evaluated to determine whether meaningful communication is taking place.

8. Written media should be developed, including bulletin boards, newsletters, letters to the homes, employee bulletins, management bulletins, policy and procedure manuals, and exhibits on employee benefits, safety, productivity, quality, attendance, suggestions, and so on.

Management must make sure that each employee knows precisely what is expected of him and that each considers this expectation fair and reasonable. Management must further insure that each employee knows exactly what he is receiving as compensation for his efforts and considers these rewards fair and equitable. Finally, management has an obligation to show employees what they can do to promote the welfare of the business—and hence their own welfare—through sound decisions and sound action in areas that are not directly job-related.

An organization is an information system. It gathers, evaluates, combines, and disseminates information. Where the success of an organization depends on the coordinated efforts of all its members, the managers are dependent on the quality and quantity of the relevant information and the rate at which it reaches them. The remainder of the organization, in turn, depends for its existence upon the efficiency with which managers can deal with this information in drawing sound conclusions and making quality decisions.

It is therefore not unreasonable to expect significant performance improvement where communication has been virtually nonexistent. There are many such directly measurable areas. Typical results could read as follows: (a) The number of suggestions received per 1,000 employees has increased from 10 to 20 a month, and the cost savings have gone up from $5,000 to $50,000 a year; (b) the submission of formal cost improvement by exempt personnel has increased from 6 to 30 a year and the dollar savings have gone up from $3,000 to $30,000 a year; (c) average daily absenteeism has been reduced from 9 percent to 4 percent.

The eighth objective was to *develop and implement a maintenance training program*. At the present time, the company averages one major machine breakdown every two weeks. The average down time is two and a half hours before the machine is back in service. The lost production time, including labor, is estimated to cost $80,000 to $90,000 a year. Close investigation reveals that there are no minimum maintenance standards, nor is there a regular preventive maintenance and inspection schedule. There have been two mechanical maintenance positions unfilled for the past three months. Of the present 22 maintenance employees, 15 are scheduled for retirement within the next three years. It is virtually impossible to hire these skills on the outside. No internal replacement candidates are available, although a number of employees have requested transfer to these classifications in writing, and there is no formal or informal maintenance training program. Eight *action steps* are indicated for this objective.

1. Obtain management approval and support of a two-year maintenance training program on a sustained basis, commencing with the transfer or hire of six trainees per year for the next two years. (Where

a union is involved, the proper notifications should be made in advance of the program to solicit their understanding and support.)

2. Determine the selection criteria, including age, education, basic skill requirements, aptitudes, attitudes, attendance, and performance on present job—quality, skill, care, effort, dependability, productivity.

3. Invite applications from the shop by announcing the program and its entrance requirements to all employees through bulletin boards, employee publications, and supervisory informative meetings.

4. Concurrent with step 3, establish a pay structure with appropriate step-rate progressions tied in with time and performance (to be determined by a series of accurate predetermined standards).

5. Review applications; first check to see whether minimum entrance requirements are met, then meet with the supervisor of each applicant to evaluate present performance and qualifications.

6. Administer aptitude and intelligence tests as appropriate to those selected.

7. Conduct a series of group interviews with the candidates to determine interest, personal qualifications, willingness to make sacrifices (long hours, heavy reading program, additional education, and evenings away from home), and so on.

8. Make final selections; obtain candidate acceptances; make major public announcements inside and outside the company; start the program on a prescheduled date.

It should be noted in the preparation for maintenance apprentice training that a number of benefits will accrue soon. Regular inspections will be scheduled; to give trainees actual on-the-job learning experiences, machines will be taken out of production for repair and overhaul *before* they break down. It has been found that the start of a new training effort like this represents a major commitment to employee training and development, and numerous other benefits are soon evident, such as reduction in the number and severity of accidents, grievances, and dissatisfactions. In actual dollar savings resulting directly from reduced scrap and breakdowns, it is reasonable to expect an annual saving of $90,000 which will more than offset the cost of the entire program, including related evening studies at a nearby vocational school.

The ninth objective is to *develop and implement a layoff and recall system for rapid upward and downward adjustments in the size of the workforce.* The business is subject to severe cyclical and seasonal variations. Although the new management information system (which plots weekly sales, shipments, billings, backlog, and inventory position) has substantially improved the predictability of these rises and declines in sales volume, management reaction in adjusting the size of the workforce has been slow—both in the timing and size of the cutbacks and in the pace of restaffing for full production. The results have been a reduction in the number of inventory turns, an increase in working investment, and inventory losses because of obsolescence and reduction. When sales volume has picked up the plant has been unable to get back into full scale production quickly enough. It is estimated that the losses owing to inventory accumulations alone amount to $150,000 a year. The object here is to provide a plan and an approach which will trigger necessary, timely workforce adjustments by communicating the need and providing the workable procedures. Five *action steps* are indicated for this objective.

1. The top sales, manufacturing, control, and human resources executives should analyze weekly information inputs to determine trends and decide on the desirability of immediate or delayed action.

2. When the decision is made to cut back or build up, a more desirable inventory and production plan should be worked out (manually or with mechanical assistance), and this plan should then be translated into numbers of people required—by job classification.

3. A goal to implement the new schedule within five working days should be considered acceptable. This will require the following actions: (a) Group like jobs into job families so as to limit the number of individual displacements and to insure that a man is transferred only into a job for which he is qualified. In all cases, ability to do the job must be the governing consideration. This ability should be determined by an individual's experience and performance and the foreman's evaluation. In cases of minimum acceptable qualifications, seniority must prevail in determining whether a man gets the job. The option of accepting or rejecting an assignment should not be available to employees on a downward displacement. (b) Production disruptions and individual displacements should be minimized with the new procedure to the extent that there will be only one displacement for every four using the past procedure. Previous adjustments required two to three weeks to establish new schedules, thus resulting in excessive penalties to the employees and to the company.

4. The employee representatives should be presented with the new procedure, and their concurrence, understanding, and support should be solicited.

5. Informative meetings should be held with all managers and supervisors of hourly rated employees to insure that the plan is properly communicated and implemented.

Given the ability, the team, and the mechanism to react more quickly to major business fluctuations, inventory turnover should go from four to six times, inventory losses should be reduced by $70,000 in the first year, and employees should experience considerably reduced losses of payroll dollars because of the reduced number of displacements. It is good business to find solutions to business problems which benefit both employer and employee. Management will find considerably less resistance to change if employee needs are factored into all management decisions.

The foregoing balanced objectives meet a number of the human resources executive's responsibilities and objectives as described in Chapter 2. Furthermore, these balanced objectives go a long way toward helping to satisfy top management's six basic concerns of recruitment, utilization, motivation, development, compensation, and retention of superior people to produce superior results.

In allocating precious managerial time, the human resources executive must establish priorities to satisfy both operating needs and people needs. His success or failure is therefore largely dependent on how he allocates his own time. He must establish the criteria for determining the validity and the priority of his objectives. Measurable profit impact cannot be excluded from these criteria.

If the responsibilities and the broad objectives outlined in Chapter 2 are properly defined in relation to business needs and people needs, all that remains is to assess the present situation and future prospects (as was done in the foregoing goals statements) and develop appropriate targets which can readily earn the full support and commitment of top management.

It is understood that while the position description of the human resources executive may vary little from year to year (as is true of an organization's broad human resource objectives) the specific goals will vary considerably as they are influenced by current internal and external events. Consider, for example, a major acquisition by the parent company. The acquired company will require a substantial investment of time from the human resources staff for a successful and complete integration of their human resources. This will include matters of policy, procedure, objectives, goals, targets, and continuing responsibilities.

The point is that goals are set from year to year and are changed and modified as business circumstances change. This is a further reason why position descriptions, broad objectives, and specific goals are needed. Traveling is easier with a roadmap.

5
Job Satisfaction, Productivity, and Profitability

Management literature is replete with praise for managing by objectives. Its virtues as a management process are repeatedly extolled. Yet relatively few companies reap the full harvest of this major breakthrough in the management of the human asset.

This is true for a variety of reasons. Some companies develop a reasonably good performance appraisal system and call this management by objectives. Other companies ask all their managers to submit a list of priorities for the coming fiscal year and report on the action taken with regard to those priorities at year-end. They call this management by objectives. Still others ask middle managers to commit themselves to a series of objectives which have been handed down from senior management with neither participation nor involvement of the people who must carry out these objectives.

The sixth objective described in Chapter 4 delineates a management-by-objectives approach to manager development. It starts with the chief executive, who works in close cooperation with his key people and stays with the program until it becomes a new way of life in his entire organization.

This chapter describes a carefully developed and well-implemented approach to managing by objectives in a large, highly diversified company. Included is a step-by-step development of the program, pointing out the pitfalls and setbacks as well as the positive direct and indirect benefits.

In our case study the impetus for management by objectives came from the president, who recognized a need to do something positive about manager development in his company and who decided to use managing by objectives as the foundation. Many of the division managers had little formal exposure to this technique, but had been reasonably successful because of superior products, market penetration, low costs, and good basic market strategy. The time was ripe for the introduction of newer and more sophisticated modern management techniques because patents were expiring, markets were evaporating, competition was becoming more intense, the businesses were becoming more complex, and there was a crying need for delegation of responsibility and identification and development of managerial talent to provide continuity in several of the divisions.

It was ascertained that no one in the company was qualified or available to initiate and implement this new approach to improving present business results while preparing tomorrow's managers today. Accordingly, a manager of executive development was recruited from outside the company to develop and implement management by objectives. The new position reported to the vice-president of personnel because this function serviced all the divisions as well as corporate staff in management of the human asset.

Pilot Project Setup

Because there was general agreement that management by objectives was a line responsibility, key line executives representing varying levels of sophistication from a good cross section of the divisions were chosen for an experimental project.

The initial participants were three division presidents, two marketing vice-presidents, two manufacturing vice-presidents, and a division controller.

To insure necessary line commitment from the outset, these executives were queried to ascertain what they felt the company's approach to a series of highly diversified operations should be so as to insure some consistency and uniformity of approach while not stifling individual entrepreneurship.

The manager of executive development was instructed to keep the project simple, concise, flexible, adaptable, readily understood, uncomplicated, not threatening. A format was developed and presented to senior management—line and staff—for review and comment before working with the pilot group. After the necessary modifications, each participant was personally visited by the manager of executive development. In advance of the meetings, each man was sent a copy of the newly developed guide and asked to think about his objectives for the coming fiscal year.

Generally, the reception to this approach was cordial; most of the pilot group felt they were already managing by objectives, but not in quite such a formal manner. Some said their goals had just been handed to them in the past and they welcomed the chance to exercise specific direction over their jobs. At least two of the top executives wanted to take the program down to the first-line supervisory level as soon as possible. One manager felt it was another chore to add to an already heavy workload. He also felt that it could be used as a whip to get every manager overcommitted and that he would not want his performance measured on the results of his performance toward his stated objectives. "The many other things I have to do well every day are at least as important as six or eight major objectives in one year."

Most managers thought the idea of having their key people involved in setting their own goals would improve results and minimize excuses and buck-passing. At least two managers felt that there was some duplication of existing programs; for example, the numbers in the annual profit plan and the forecasts for the annual management meeting. There was also the matter of long-range planning (in this company, three years), which had been initiated within the preceding year. These comments were carefully noted for use in putting the final package together as part of every manager's personal and professional development.

On the basis of all the inputs, a tailor-made flexible approach was evolved giving each division manager plenty of latitude on how he would apply management by objectives in his particular job and how far and how fast he would carry the approach down throughout his organization. The formal performance appraisal was omitted for the first year, and an informal annual progress review was substituted in its place.

The first year's performance against objectives was not to affect any individual's compensation, thus allowing time for the men to adapt to this new way of working and recognizing the importance of superior day-to-day application of business fundamentals. Certain specific guidelines were developed, however, for use by the division manager and his key people in formulating an approach tailored to his division's needs. The group executive to whom the division managers reported was also requested to prepare a statement on management by objectives. Guidelines were suggested in six areas.

1. *Statement of problems and opportunities*. Beginning with the chief executive, each manager was requested to prepare a concise written statement of the major problem and opportunity areas facing his operations in the coming year. This was done to facilitate allocating priorities to the areas of greatest need and keeping them in focus during the coming year. A typical statement of problems and opportunities came from the container group.

> The major challenge facing the container group is to integrate the organization under one common management. While the integration

necessitates close, cohesive teamwork to realize the full benefits of the large-scale organization, it also mandates retention of the uniqueness and individual entrepreneurship which enabled each of the four companies to command a prime position in their respective markets.

The key problem areas, then, involve organization structuring, staffing, and determining the most beneficial working relationships to achieve the advantages of size while maintaining the advantages of individuality and uniqueness.

Through the creation of permanent interlocking groups from among general and functional management in each of the four glass container companies, the business will, in a short time, be in a position to improve operating results while providing for future growth and diversification. These cohesive groups include the president's operating committee and the technical, financial, marketing, manufacturing, and industrial relations committees.

As an example of what could be done through this cooperative effort, the total market situation could be carefully observed to avoid overproduction or shortages. Soft spots in demand would be more readily detected through the combined professional skills of the vice-presidents of marketing utilizing modern management techniques.

Numerous other opportunities exist within these groups, such as optimum use of human and material resources, including facilities and equipment, which should measurably benefit the container group. The first year presents a unique opportunity for consolidation, integration, and organization to make the whole greater than the sum of its parts.

2. *Listing of major responsibility areas, emphasizing priorities.* Recognizing that formal position descriptions existed for only a few key managerial positions, each manager was asked to concentrate his attention on the six to eight major responsibilities of his position, emphasizing priority of importance, but not necessarily in priority order. If a responsibility was important enough to put on paper, it was important enough to merit attention in the coming year, but the degree of importance and emphasis should shift from one year to the next.

In effect, this step amounted to the formulation of a brief yet meaningful position description for each managerial job. Sample position descriptions are to be found in the Appendix.

Given the statements of problems, opportunities, and position responsibilities, the manager was now ready to formulate his specific goals—bearing in mind the need to relate them to the overall corporate objectives.

Some managers felt at this point that they should have a goal for each major area of responsibility; others did not think this was necessary. The consensus was to leave this to the discretion of the division manager, noting that there usually are one or two areas which require relatively little attention in any one year.

3. *Development of specific goals statements.* To help each manager insure that each goal represented a meaningful contribution to business results, a number of suggested criteria and considerations for effective goals statements were developed. Among the questions for *general management* to consider were these. Is there a goal for each major segment of the business? Are organization and structure satisfactory? Are there capable managers in all key positions? Are backup candidates identified? What about administration? Business plan? Plans for acquisition, divestiture, new product lines, phasing out of product lines?

Questions for *marketing management* consideration included these. What is the volume of sales in total, by geographic region, and by salesman? What is the share of market and/or market segment? Are the market plan and strategy adequate, timely, useful? What are the possible new markets for entry? Has exposure been assessed? What about distributor channels? Warehousing? Freight costs? Product planning and development? Product pricing? Sales coverage? Product mix?

These were some of the questions for *manufacturing management* consideration. What are the capital expenditure requirements for facilities and equipment? Is the manufacturing capacity adequate? What changes are anticipated in technology, processes, materials, or products? Has the impact on present operations and costs been assessed? What plans have been made for improvement of manufacturing efficiencies, standards, indirect labor, materials? What are the anticipated needs and changes in organization and personnel? Are controls adequate? Is the management information system adequate? Is the production and inventory control system adequate? Are quality levels and standards competitive? Are quality costs properly identified and assessed?

Questions for *finance and controls* included these. Is information about return on investment available by plant, by product, by item, and by cost center? Is it satisfactory? Is the number of inventory turns acceptable? What is the accounts receivable status? Does the cost system provide sufficient, timely information? Do departmental budgets receive proper attention? Are they sufficiently controlled? Is a profitability analysis by customer available? Any delays in paperwork processing, reports, and so on?

Among the *personnel* questions were these. What are the labor problems—negotiations, probable work stoppages, and so on? Is the labor supply adequate? What is its quality? Are there any special training or orientation requirements? What is the status of turnover at all levels (voluntary resignations)? Comparative safety and accident statistics? Training time and induction procedures? Recruiting costs? Quality and results of training and developmental projects, including a backup man, and replacement planning? Social, political, and economic climates?

Whenever possible, each goal had to represent a specific, measurable result to be achieved. It was to be stated in quantified terms such as dollars or tons or percentage of improvement.

Where goals could not be quantified—the improvement of a management information system, the installation of a standard cost system, or the initiation and implementation of a key man backup project, for example—specific timetables were established and used as one of the bases for evaluation of results.

A division manager's goals could include any major area of significant impact on business results, even though he was not going to do the work himself. Typical goals would cover the resolution of a major quality problem, the recruitment of a key executive, the improvement of labor relations. It was assumed that in most instances, there would be at least one goal for each major function of the business.

The managers understood that their goals should take cognizance of listed problem and opportunity areas; identify performance standards and suggest measurements; complement and support corporate objectives and related goals at the same organizational level; be realistic, practical, and attainable; cause the individual to stretch and develop by pinpointing his developmental needs and providing for his accelerated growth; build in provision for communication and interrelating of goals with those primarily involved and/or affected; provide checkpoints for review and discussion.

Typical goals statements are shown in Exhibit 5-1.

4. *Implementation.* To implement this flexible approach, a task force of line executives was freed of other responsibilities so they could devote their full time and attention to the program. The men appointed were of such caliber as to make it clear to everyone in the organization that top management intended to have management by objectives become a way of life. The human resources executive served as a consultant to help line executives install and monitor the program. Other corporate staff assistance was made available on request both in the initial formulation of goals statements and in the realization of these goals.

Often overlooked in this initial phase is the importance of the manager-man relationship. This will make or break management by objectives, because the manager's sincerity in delegating significant decision-making responsibility and authority as opposed to token participation, providing counsel and coaching in helping the man to formulate

Exhibit 5-1.
A TYPICAL DIVISION'S MANAGEMENT-BY-OBJECTIVES GOALS PLAN

Statement of Problems and Opportunities

The division's growth rate is approximately 18% per year. Prior marketing emphasis has been on volume selling with little attention directed to analyses of product and customer profitability. The result has been acceptance of some business with less than satisfactory margins.

Our plant expansion program will increase our productive capacity by 30%. This fact, coupled with the current sellers' market, presents an opportunity to shift the marketing strategy to selective selling and hence a maximization of profit on new business. The division's recently acquired franchise as a supplier of specialty containers presents an immediate growth opportunity. We will aggressively seek a larger share of this market segment.

Company growth has also necessitated a restructuring of our organization including the reassignment of key individuals and revision of position responsibilities. Problems of unfavorable inventory variances caused by inadequate production and inventory control systems will be corrected by reorganizing the function and staffing it with a qualified individual.

Briefly, this year is characterized by rapid and substantial growth. Facilities, organization, systems, controls, and people are being developed to solve the problems and take advantage of the opportunities presented by the present market situation.

Operational Goals

1. Increase sales from $13,122,000 to $17,009,000 (30%).
2. Improve return on investment from 12% to 15%.
3. Increase net profit from $1,506,000 to $2,362,000.
4. Achieve payback calculated on capital expenditure on time and within budget.

Manufacturing Goals

1. Increase productive capacity 30% by having the new facility on stream by June 15.
2. Increase productive efficiency by 3%.
3. Reduce man-hours per ton from 9.7 to 9.0.
4. Refine production and inventory control systems to improve the balance between customer satisfaction and manufacturing efficiency and company profitability.

Marketing Goals

1. Develop yardsticks to measure the effects of selective selling by product and customer profitability by June 1 to permit the establishment of quantitative goals.

2. Implement the program of selective selling to effect a 15% increase in profit on net sales by December 1.
3. Increase special order sales from 259,000 units to 559,000 units.
4. Evaluate the desirability of continued participation in the brokerage business and make a decision by year-end.

Management and Organization Goals

1. Restructure the company organization and realign positions and individuals by year-end to realize full benefit from the expansion program.
2. Identify key high-potential management personnel and plan programs by year-end to accelerate their development.
3. Continue the in-house management development program utilizing internal and external professional capabilities.
4. Implement a manpower inventory by September 30.
5. Insure that all key positions are staffed with qualified individuals by year-end.

Quality Goals

1. Develop yardsticks for measuring the degree of customer satisfaction to permit establishment of quantitative goals.
2. Develop a plan for the establishment of a central quality control organization by year-end.

Administration Goals

1. Develop ways and means of utilizing the standard cost system to improve managerial effectiveness in planning and control of operations.

Employee Relations Goals

1. Reduce turnover from 80% to 60%.
2. Develop a safety program that will result in reductions of accident frequency and severity rates.
3. Increase number of applicants accepted under the JOBS program to a full commitment of five.

External Relations Goals

1. Arrange for the division manager to visit the ten major customers at least once a year.
2. Continue active participation in community affairs and professional organizations.

Future Growth Goals

1. Develop plans for construction and use of a new office building.
2. Evaluate present machinery and equipment in terms of technological competitiveness and make appropriate recommendations.
3. Develop a chart of future capital projects establishing priorities and target dates for their completion.

his goals, and removing obstructions to goal attainment—all these will help or hinder a man's on-the-job development. On the other hand, in formulating his goals the individual must be fully prepared to review the specific action he and others must take, and the time when they must take it, to achieve each goal. He should also be prepared to suggest interim and final measures to assess his contribution to business effectiveness as well as to his own development.

The final goals statement must represent a joint commitment of the man and his manager—a psychological contract, if you will—to achieve the man's goals. If the man fails, the good manager understands that he, too, has failed at some point along the way.

All statements of goals should have the full concurrence and support of the next two higher levels of management and the concurrence of managers at the same organizational level in other functions if they are in any way involved or affected by the outcome. This serves a twofold purpose; first, to let senior management know who the star performers are and hence the candidates for additional accelerated development; second, to insure that all executives on the same level are emphasizing the same basic priorities properly tied together at the top. If the engineering department is stressing basic research and the marketing department is emphasizing the sales of new products, the organization suffers. Goals and objectives must be compatible with each other.

The company in our case study counted it particularly important to hold informal progress reviews on a man-to-man basis at natural break points in time—initially, every three months to provide early warning of unrealistic or unattainable goals which could be catastrophic. For example, it would be disastrous to maintain full production despite a sudden and rapid decline in sales or fail to reduce costs and expenses in line with reduced revenue.

In these progress reviews, format and technique were deemed far less important than a manager's demonstrated willingness to help a man achieve his goals. These were positive, problem-identification-and-correction sessions with the manager serving as coach and counselor rather than critic or judge and jury.

One caution: There is more to management by objectives than merely finishing a task on time, and deadlines should not be the sole criteria for successful performance. Nor should the measures be subjective or be used as a means of trapping the man. One purpose of managing by objectives is to help the man toward self-actualization, not to hinder or harass him. In this same light, an overemphasis on words and format is to be avoided. The idea is to obtain acceptance of the concept through ease and simplicity of face-to-face communication.

5. *Evaluation of results.* Management by objectives highlighted a number of areas which needed attention. Specifically—

- There was duplication among annual profit planning, long-range planning, and management by objectives.
- A number of executives experienced difficulty in defining problems, opportunities, and major responsibilities. Often their concepts of priorities differed from those of their managers.
- A number of existing good management practices were brought to light and made available to other managers.
- Some managers tried to move too fast and a few people were overwhelmed at first.
- Those managers who declined to participate or gave only half-hearted support showed the poorest operating results.
- Duplication of effort and unclear assignments were uncovered.
- The shortage of real management depth was readily apparent.
- Most managers wanted to know how well they were doing and how to improve their performance, but relatively few were given this information. Yet their managers were sure that each man knew where he stood.
- Several managers felt that if given another opportunity they could improve their performance.
- Some managers believed that there was little relationship between compensation and contribution to business results.

The group which fully implemented MBO accounted for one-quarter of the sales and a much greater percentage of total company profits.

6. *Follow-up.* It was decided to retain management by objectives as a permanent approach to management. To avoid duplication yet provide for healthy overlap, the program was incorporated into the annual profit planning process. This provided the narrative support and delineation of action steps required to support the profit plan. It additionally allowed for incorporation of nonnumerical goals such as manager development and performance appraisal. The approach to performance appraisal consisted of *periodic reviews of progress.* Periodic review and discussion of work plan progress between man and manager is conducive to more effective individual contribution. Such reviews were recommended in relation to each individual planned item at natural break points, such as project stages, project completion, or quarterly budgetary periods and also whenever man or manager felt it desirable between these break points.

The primary reason for such reviews and discussions—the feedback of performance results—is to stimulate development and improve work performance. To be most effective, feedback should follow close on the heels of the employee's actions. If the feedback is favorable, it will reinforce action; if unfavorable, it will permit rapid adjustment of action. Learning experiments show that when feedback is delayed, much of the impetus to learning is lost. Therefore, review and discussion of progress should not be withheld until the annual appraisal, but conducted as soon as a piece of work is finished. The formal annual appraisal may then be used for a general review of performance and, of special importance, for looking ahead and making revisions in work plans.

The feedback of performance results at any time should be (1) positive and constructive rather than negative, (2) specific rather than general, (3) translated into actions for the future, (4) work-oriented, not focused on personality, and (5) an addition to what the employee already knows. It is only proper, then, that periodic progress reviews and discussions should cover four points:

1. *Review* of performance reflected in progress on planned items and discussion of situational factors affecting progress.
2. *Counsel* by the managers on possible alternate ways of solving problems.
3. *Agreement* on what projects and other items are going well and those in need of more attention or action.
4. *Revision,* as necessary, of individual items and results to be achieved during specified periods.

Periodic review and counseling is intended not to replace but to supplement day-to-day working relationships. It places emphasis on full participation by both man and manager. Both must be prepared for free discussion—without the manager's feeling that he must rate overall performance at that time.

To help improve individual effectiveness, attention should be given by both the man and the manager to underlying factors—(1) those arising from the job situation, (2) those that are due to the manager himself, and (3) those that are traceable to the individual. An analysis of these factors must precede any constructive suggestions for changes or actions.

The degree to which a manager may elect to utilize periodic reviews will vary with individuals and specific circumstances. It is important, however, not only that each individual have a copy of his current work plan, but that he be free to request a progress review whenever he feels one is desirable. In evaluating performance results during periodic progress reviews a separate performance review sheet such as the one shown in Exhibit 5-2 should be completed by each man.

Exhibit 5-2.
SAMPLE PERFORMANCE REVIEW FORMAT

Man	Manager	
Self-appraisal of responsibilities	Comments	Major objectives and plans for next year
(Consider especially those responsibilities where major objectives were not assigned, those involving integration relationships, etc.)	(Consider significant differences of opinion, additional interpretative comments, etc.)	
Self-appraisal on accomplishment of objectives		Comments
(Consider results generated in terms of quality, quantity, timeliness, cost, creativity. Areas needing additional or less attention. Roadblocks faced.)		
		For time period from:____ To:____ Man:______________ Manager:__________ Date of Review:______

Note: To be completed independently by the man and his manager, in pencil, for discussion purposes.

Actually, a total corporate planning system was evolved by the company in our case study; it incorporated and simplified long-range planning, annual profit planning, and the best of management by objectives. A corporate model plan was developed which included all major division projects in priority order of importance relative to short-term profitability and long-term growth.

Other results are worthy of note. Communication was significantly improved, both within line operations and between line and staff operations. Fuzzy assignments were cleared up. The four division managers who chose to carry the program down through the next two or three organizational layers experienced better operating results than their counterparts who did not; in two cases, profit plan figures were exceeded. Individual managerial strengths and limitations were identified and specific developmental efforts were initiated. More attention was paid to organization and manpower planning to the degree that key staff personnel at the line operating level were added to fill organization voids. Superior people were hired to fill open positions. The new criterion was whether a man had the potential to advance two levels beyond the present assignment.

Nor was this all. Manager development took its rightful place as a major agenda item for subsequent business policy meetings and the annual key manager meetings. Key managers were brought together more frequently. A companywide performance appraisal system was developed. Compensation practices began to move away from uniform increases and become more directly related to accomplishment. Marginal performers were clearly identified and appropriate measures were taken to strengthen performance. Voluntary resignations of line operating executives were reduced. Ten divisions which had not held first-line supervisory training sessions implemented those programs. A key backup man project was begun at the top management level and implemented through the division manager level. And plans were made to go to the next two lower levels of management in the line and staff operations.

While it could be argued that many of the foregoing benefits might have happened anyway, the fact is that they had not. Management by objectives served as a stimulus because it let exempt people know that top management was very much aware of their existence and that this awareness was accompanied by a genuine interest in individual career development. It proved that broad corporate objectives can become personalized and meaningful to the individual. Furthermore, it demonstrated that job satisfaction increases productivity, which in turn increases profitability.

While it took more than a year to reap the benefits of implementing management by objectives at the top of the organization, this success insured continuity, whereas starting out at the middle or lower management levels is almost predestined for failure because of a lack of compatibility and kinship with top management philosophies, values, attitudes, and objectives.

A results-oriented approach to manager development brings to the individual an accurate picture of the business, his specific opportunities for contribution, and the necessary responsibility and authority to realize and demonstrate his full potential for growth and development. Management by objectives meets individual needs and realizes business objectives. It insures commitment, involvement, and lasting personal satisfaction.

6
The Manager and His Human Resources

A good manager plans, organizes, leads, controls, and measures. He blends these activities with generous doses of communication. In discharging his responsibilities, he must not limit his consideration solely to material, financial, and physical assets. That this would be an exercise in futility has been evidenced by the staggering number of managerial failures resulting from poor interpersonal relationships. Much has been said and written about the management of physical, financial, and material assets, but too little attention has focused on what concerns us here—the human asset, a manager's most valuable resource.

The human resources executive has the responsibility to teach managers the full scope of their stewardship responsibility in planning for, selecting, utilizing, motivating, developing, compensating, and retaining their human assets. Accountability must be defined, provided for, and measured within the framework of legitimate business objectives and not as the fulfillment of a personnel department requirement.

Managing is a distinct kind of work. It involves the administration of the business enterprise, or a segment thereof, to achieve its objectives through effective leadership of its personnel.

It has been pointed out that the most effective leadership is achieved through inspiring, encouraging, teaching, and motivating all employees to perform well and enthusiastically, but within the framework of an integrated and synchronized business team. This is what the term *synergy* is all about—collectively, the group produces results far superior to those which could be produced by the individuals separately, regardless of effort. Manpower must be integrated with money, materials, and machines to generate the best results in realizing the objectives of the enterprise.

Through proper planning for and systematic selection and development of competent managerial personnel, the organization can insure its continuity and profitability and progress. To do this, there must exist a clear and soundly designed organization structure along with concisely expressed policies, fully implemented. The abilities, resourcefulness, and initiative of all personnel at all levels can be released to achieve excellence in teamwork if they are encouraged by appropriate financial and nonfinancial incentives which are proportionate to their individual responsibilities, risks, and achievements.

Planning Human Resource Needs

A manager's planning encompasses all resources of the business or the component for which he is responsible. This includes the human resource. Most managers establish objectives; the process has already been described. Human resource objectives are a vital part of this managerial job. Good managers recognize that the quality, availability, and use of human resources determine the quality, scope, and character of the objectives as well as their realization. They also limit the number of alternative courses of action that can be considered. Clear-cut objectives avoid confusion, rigidity, and stagnation. They evidence flexibility; they permit change and progress; they anticipate the future creatively and constructively.

Just as all managers are active in goal setting, they also are active in establishing and implementing policy. Sound policies reflect a broad understanding of human values. They help to keep good perspective and balance between short-term and long-range goals as well as between jobs in each department, and between the departments and the company as a whole. Written policies provide guidelines on matters of major importance to the whole organization wherever consistency of action is necessary and desirable. Policies are needed to avoid making the same decisions over and over again.

Policies help to determine managerial priorities as well as maintain a realistic balance among specific objectives. They help to resolve conflicts of interest. Properly implemented, they anticipate obstacles or difficulties and thus leave managers better prepared to deal with them. Expressed policies, properly communicated, help to generate loyalty and understanding inside and outside the company.

Personnel or employee relations policies provide an excellent foundation for a manager's approach to human resource management. The human resources executive takes the initiative in formulating such policy, but he consults with senior managers to get their reactions and approval because, in the final analysis, it is the line managers who must live with and implement employee relations policies.

Typical employee relations policies cover organization structure, position descriptions, recruitment and employment, physical examinations, manager development, orientation and induction, exempt overtime payments, conflicts of interest, submitted ideas, employee incentives, promotions and transfers, transfer allowances, relocation expenses, communication, government inquiries, publications, drugs and alcohol, public service, educational assistance, compensation, managerial awards, manpower reviews, performance standards, vacations, benefits, security, employee dissatisfactions, personnel and union relations, discipline and discharge, social responsibility, employee surveys, exit interviews, and performance appraisal.

Policies need not be complex; simple statements will usually suffice. If an explanation or implementation is required, it should be part of the policy. (Examples are included in the Appendix.) In areas represented by the foregoing list, the absence of written policy can lead to confusion. It creates difficulties in developing teamwork and results in inconsistent treatment of employees at all levels. The absence of written and properly communicated and enforced policy is a major sign that an organization has human relations problems. The larger the organization, the more intense the need for spelled-out policies.

It is not sufficient merely to develop a set of policy statements and let them gather dust. At least annually, all policies should be reviewed by all managers who must implement them. The human resources executive should solicit their comments (preferably in advance of a prescheduled meeting with senior management) for suggestions on new policy needs, revision and updating of present policy to fit changing conditions, review of infractions and effectiveness of implementation, new or revised procedures to insure compliance, and discussion of ways to discourage circumvention and encourage enforcement.

It has been found that in many enterprises only a few copies of policy manuals exist, and managers and supervisors who have direct accountability for implementation have no access to the manuals. In most cases, enlarging the distribution lists could well improve employee understanding.

Each manager should be encouraged to set aside one-half day a year to meet with all his exempt employees in small groups to review policy matters and related considerations. Each employee should prepare for these meetings well in advance, particularly with regard to policy areas that directly affect him, his people, and his ability to meet his objectives. During the meetings, participants should raise questions in depth on any aspect of policy formulation, administration, or implementation.

Finally, it should be recognized that statements of policy which are transmitted by word of mouth are subject to gross misunderstanding and misapplication. The farther down the line these interpretations of policy are transmitted, the greater the likelihood of distortion in meaning and intent. There is no substitute for first-hand information and a copy of the written policy.

Other aspects of planning include the actual selection and statement of tasks required to accomplish objectives, as was described in Chapter 4. To achieve his goals, every manager needs to determine his programs, including priorities and time schedules. These must be so succinctly stated that all employees can visualize what is required and participate in getting the job done.

These programs will go nowhere until quality, quantity, and timing of manpower needs—particularly managerial and professional—are expressed and translated into manpower budgets. A manager's manpower plans and budgets must include financial support for in-house and outside development of individual managerial and professional employees. It must factor in replenishment needs and recruitment and training of lower-level supervisors, apprentices, and others. A long-range plan is incomplete without a personnel section as illustrated in Exhibit 6-1. There must also be a plan for measuring performance of individuals and operations. This will be developed in detail later.

Organizing to Maximize Productivity and Satisfaction

Organizing and planning are linked in many ways and mutually dependent. The main difference is that planning concerns itself with deciding what work is to be done while organizing concerns itself primarily with the arrangements for getting it done.

From a human resource utilization viewpoint, it is necessary for managers to raise a number of questions: What needs to be accomplished, and why? When must it be done, and where is the best place to do it? What are the logical classifications into which the work must be divided? What form of organization will provide the best arrangement of human resources to accomplish this job? What positions are needed? Who will do the work? What relationships, formal and informal, need to be integrated and communicated to insure cohesive teamwork and interrelationship of goals?

Every manager wants to have a good working climate—to have a group of employees who are motivated to achieve business goals and accept them as their personal goals. The creation of this environment is largely dependent upon the manager's interpersonal skills; in such a climate each individual assumes complete responsibility not only for doing his own job to the best of his ability, but also for integrating his efforts with those of all other individuals who affect his work or are affected by it.

Every act of management requires a cooperative relationship between two or more persons for its successful consummation. A unity of purpose produces the most productive working climate.

The organization structure itself has a profound effect on people's attitudes toward their work. Organization structure, in its broadest sense, includes all the working relationships within the organization—all the individual and collective responsibilities, whether specifically indicated or not.

To a given manager, the formal organization represents what is expected from his personal output. He relates to others in terms of who works on what, when, and why as well as who is dependent on whom for the flow of work. Even a position title implies an understanding of duties, responsibilities, and relationships.

All this serves to stress the fact that every manager needs to plan his segment of the organization in accord with the overall structure. If it is allowed to evolve by itself, many of the concerns expressed earlier will become real problems. When the organization is well planned, more work can be done at less cost because people will know what is expected of them as well as why it needs to be done.

Every manager has a natural tendency to concentrate on short-term results; this is usually the primary basis on which he is compensated and promoted. The human resources executive must convince top management that by giving balanced attention to the future through development of human resources, today's work will not suffer, but will actually improve. If tomorrow is not planned for, it may find everyone unprepared when it comes.

Basing an organization on sound planning helps to prevent the crises of unforeseen personnel needs on the one hand and the sudden unexpected shortage of some specialized talent on the other hand.

The difference between making things happen and just allowing them to happen is accounted for by good organization planning. When people are confused as to what is expected of them and of others with whom they work, they miss opportunities and are slow to react to problems. Both situations are dealt with more quickly when everyone knows what is expected of him and what to expect from others.

Managers must be sensitive to the needs of people. It has already been stressed that most people *want* to do a good job; they *want* to learn, to grow, to improve their lot. But their viewpoints must be respected. The right organization structure helps to provide this climate of motivation in which people do the excellent work that they want to do anyway.

Exhibit 6-1.
PERSONNEL SECTION OF THE LONG-RANGE MANPOWER PLAN

Because the management of our human resources is a vital factor in achieving the long-range plan, this section is included to identify those critical present and future employee relations considerations, including manpower supply and demand, which could have an impact on our ability to realize long-range goals.

Organization Charts

Attach a copy of your current organization chart and your three-year projected organization chart. The projected chart should identify all new positions to be added and positions which will have changed substantially because of addition or deletion of product lines, expansion or contraction of the business, creation of new functions (director of planning, manager of information systems, director of research and development, for example).

For each new position to be added and each position to be substantially changed, the appropriate manager should prepare a list of the eight to ten major responsibilities with emphasis on priority of importance.

Projected Manpower Requirements

	Annual Projections											
	EXEMPT BONUS			EXEMPT NONBONUS			NONEXEMPT SALARIED			HOURLY		
Functions	1st	2d	3d	1st	2d	3d	1st	2d	3d	1st	2d	3d
Finance and accounting												
Marketing and sales												
Manufacturing												
Employee relations												
Administration												
Product engineering												

How Anticipated Openings Will Be Filled (exempt bonus only)

1. Positions to be filled from outside company: *Date Required*

______________________ ______________

2. Positions to be filled by promotion from within: Approximate Date

______________________ ______________

Compensation

	Anticipated percent and dollar increases in compensation					
	1st year		2d year		3d year	
	Percent	Dollars	Percent	Dollars	Percent	Dollars
Exempt bonus	______	$______	______	$______	______	$______
Exempt nonbonus	______	______	______	______	______	______
Nonexempt salary	______	______	______	______	______	______
Hourly	______	______	______	______	______	______

Local Labor Market and Business Conditions

Identify any unusual local plant community conditions affecting your human resources, whether social, economical, political, labor, or environmental, which could materially affect your division's ability to realize its long-range objectives. Identify each problem and opportunity and discuss what your plans are to minimize or eliminate the problems and take full advantage of the opportunities.

Such conditions might include a militant union, tight labor supply, entry or departure of businesses, union organization attempt, possible effects of anticipated changes in your business or other businesses in the area.

The good organization structure is logical. This means that, to be good, it must make sense to those who live with it. It would be logical, for example, to place production planning and control, plant layout, industrial engineering, quality control, and materials management in a reporting relationship with the vice-president in charge of manufacturing, not the personnel director.

A well-planned organizational structure is understandable. It is clear, simple, and uncomplicated. It is easily communicated, and relationships are clearly defined. It is explicit.

The human resources executive needs to teach and stress and reinforce the belief in and practice of the following basic principles:

- Each individual must report to only one manager.
- There should be as few levels as possible in the structure (six to eight is a good guideline).
- The span of managerial control must be in accord with the complexity of the work to be managed and the relationship of the positions that report to the manager.

- Each position must have responsibility for specific measurable results.
- Performance results must first be fed back to the individuals who do the work.
- Positions with unclear responsibilities should be eliminated.

Organization structures must be sufficiently stable to make individual career planning possible for a reasonable period of time. A well-understood, reasonably stable structure provides a framework within which people can carry on in the event of sudden loss of their manager. In all too many situations, organizations have fallen apart with the death of the top men. These men had not communicated their knowledge of the business to anyone.

On the other hand, the structure must be sufficiently flexible to let people react quickly to unanticipated problems and take full advantage of opportunities as they present themselves. It should enable the rapid formation of a task force or project team to meet a new competitive challenge.

People normally resist change because it produces anxiety—and because they are kept in the dark as to how the changes will affect them. A good manager builds a record of smoothly executed changes. There are usually good reasons for making changes in jobs, organization, working relationships, location. These are necessary to adjust to business, social, economic, or political conditions, to meet competitive pressures, to develop new markets, to introduce new products. When employees are informed in advance (where practical and appropriate to do so), when they know they have been dealt with fairly in the past and will be treated fairly and kept informed, they will accept change without fear—as a way of life.

Formulating Position Descriptions

Part of organizing involves grouping of components of like work into position descriptions. The biggest single advantage of position descriptions is that they make more effective use of human resources to accomplish business objectives. The same benefits (including elimination of unclear assignments, duplication, and overlap) which result from sound organization structure result from well-defined position responsibilities.

A position description may more properly be termed a performance description because a good one suggests the measures of accountability as well as defining the responsibility and authority. It is urged that each manager and individual professional employee prepare his own description. It should, of course, be reviewed and approved by his boss.

An example of an actual position description for a vice-president–marketing is shown in Exhibit 6-2. Note that if a position cannot be described in terms of value added to the business, the need for that position is questionable.

Exhibit 6-2.
SAMPLE POSITION DESCRIPTION

Position title: Vice-president–marketing

Broad function: Formulate and recommend short- and long-range objectives for the company in terms of products, customers, distribution channels, prices, and marketing services. Formulate, execute, and measure realization of marketing plans and programs necessary to achieve those objectives. Achieve optimum profitability, product leadership, and market position within the limits of company objectives and operating budgets.

Reports to: President

Principal Responsibilities:

1. Advise and counsel the company president on marketing objectives, sales and service programs and policies, organization plans, budgets, product planning, production requirements, and scheduling.
2. Plan and direct the overall marketing program, including national advertising, market research, product service requirements and programs, and order service budgets and measurements to meet established volume, profit, and product goals.
3. Establish regional sales budgets by product line.
4. Analyze and evaluate the products and programs of competitors.
5. Establish and test product pricing to realize the company's profit objectives.
6. Investigate possibilities for product line broadening; direct the field analysis of new products and recommend the discontinuation of unprofitable products.
7. Provide sales, advertising, and sales promotion activities.
8. Coordinate marketing programs and activities with all other functional areas of the business to insure meeting objectives of service, delivery, quality, price, and resolution of problems.
9. Determine the organization and manpower required to carry out the marketing program and select and develop staff of qualified personnel.
10. Originate operating and activities budgets and control marketing activities within those budgets.

Decentralization

The human resources executive notes that every position represents a delegation of responsibility. This delegation must be full and complete. It must represent decentralization of responsibility, authority, and accountability. Delegation is the most difficult task for a new manager. The transition from individual contributor to manager is rugged—particularly when the manager has been an outstanding specialist. Most managers do not fully delegate; a few actually abdicate responsibility.

Yet it is here that managers can obtain the best results or fail miserably. Decentralization places authority nearest to the action. It achieves best results if the problem is understood in light of thorough knowledge of the facts. The point is that real authority must be delegated, not merely the collecting of data for review and checking with the boss. Managers must learn to put their trust in men who have the capacity to make sound decisions. Their top executives must share this belief. It is a fact that the aggregate of many individually made sound decisions is better than decisions which are planned, controlled, and made centrally. A top executive once said that he views his weekly staff meetings as "opportunities to take advantage of the collective wisdom of 200 years of experience"; he has no monopoly on brain power. The role of staff personnel is to advise and counsel the line people who make the decisions. Decentralization is effective when the general business objectives, policies, organization structure, and relationships are clearly defined and communicated. The idea works well if people at all levels fully accept and exercise responsibility and commensurate authority. And finally, performance must be accurately measured; standards must be applied consistently, and managers who do not come up to expectations must be removed from their positions.

Selection and Recruitment

To make decentralization work, managers must hire superior people at all levels of the organization. Compensation policy must be geared to pay more than the average of comparable companies competing for the highest caliber executives. Assuming that compensation is competitive, the task of the human resources executive is to help each manager improve his batting average for acceptance of job offers.

The most effective and least costly way to do this is through a selection workshop, led by the human resources executive, for key managers who have heavy recruiting needs. The following outline was used in a two-day workshop on filling jobs in a tight market.

Session I

I. WELCOME AND INTRODUCTION

A. Opening remarks

1. *Outline of workshop schedule and operating procedure.*
2. *Workshop objectives.*
   a. Understand the selection process.
   b. Review the manager's part in it.
   c. Practice selection skills within the framework of an actual job opening.
3. *The job market today.*
   a. Difficulty in finding candidates who can meet high standards.
   b. Current situation.
4. *Recruiting problems in a tight market.*

B. The selection process

1. *The state of the market.*
   a. Fierce competition for really able people.
   b. Need to convince the promising candidate.
   c. Need to adapt the job to fit the man and help him learn the things he must know.

C. The decision process

1. *Manager's limited choices.*
   a. Reject candidates who will not perform above some minimum level.
   b. Consider candidates who will.
   c. Choose one; make offer.
2. *Choices are between predictions.*
   a. What the job is and how it will change.
   b. What the conditions are and how they may change.
   c. What satisfactory performance on the job is.
   d. How the candidate will perform under pressure.
3. *Predictions about candidates.*
   a. How the candidate will perform and how he will respond to changes in job or situation.
   b. How the candidate performed on similar jobs in similar situations and how he reacted to similar changes.
   c. Source of information: interviews with candidate and his managers.

4. *The selection.*
   a. Recognize that precise predictions are impossible.
   b. Determine degree of similarity between man's past behavior and the behavior required on the job.
   c. Try to get information based on observation rather than inference.
   d. Try to learn patterns of the man's behavior that are fixed and patterns that are changeable.
   e. Identify and assess the risks.
   f. Try to know how our own biases may affect our predictions.
5. *Review of selection steps.*
   a. Defining the job.
   b. Deciding what we need to know.
   c. Identifying the sources.
   d. Collecting the information.
   e. Matching job and information.
   f. Making a choice.

II. TOUGHEST SELECTION PROBLEMS

A. Ask managers what selection problems are most troublesome. Expect them to mention:

1. *Defining the job requirements.*
2. *Making predictions when the candidate has had no experience*
3. *Evaluating aggressiveness or other personality traits.*
4. *Getting accurate information from candidates.*
5. *Getting complete information from candidates.*
6. *Getting reliable reports from former managers.*

B. Group like problems and relate them to 5 *a, b, c,* and *d* of the decision process discussed earlier.

III. WHAT THE OPENING IS REALLY LIKE

A. Disadvantages of position guide, man specs, and job specs.

B. Alternate suggestion for preparing a description of a job opening.

1. *Indicate top priority results wanted from the man who fills the job.*
2. *Identify major tasks.*
3. *Spell out critical conditions under which results must be produced.*
4. *Indicate information needed about each candidate's background.*

IV. WHAT THE CANDIDATE HAS TO OFFER

A. The employment interview

B. How to set the stage

1. *Make sure the interview is private.*
2. *Use your voice and your face to convey interest in everything he is saying.*
3. *Be yourself.*

C. Information to collect

1. *What candidate has done.*
2. *The conditions under which he did it.*
3. *Where he wants to go.*

D. Mechanics of getting information

1. *Use small talk.*
2. *Express interest in matching man and job.*
3. *Tell him why you are trying to fill the job.*
4. *Open up with a big question.*
5. *Encourage him to keep talking.*
   a. Keep quite.
   b. Use "I see" and "uh huh."
   c. Use pregnant pauses.
   d. Give pats on the back.
   e. Play down unfavorable information.
6. *Use probes.*
   a. Open-end remarks.
   b. Remarks that encourage elaboration.
   c. Comments rather than questions.
7. *Control the interview.*

V. PRACTICE INTERVIEWS

A. Break into groups of three each: interviewer, interviewee, and observer.

B. Focus on work experience part of interview.

VI. THE RÉSUMÉ

A. Caveat: Résumés sometimes are more sales pieces than anything else, so they are to be used with caution.

B. Preparation for the interview: résumés help—

1. *Screen out people.*
2. *Produce clues about areas to probe.*
3. *Select questions to ask.*
4. *Determine patterns.*

VII. INTERVIEWING FORMER MANAGERS

A. Getting the facts about the candidate.

1. *What he did.*
2. *How well he did it.*
3. *Under what conditions.*
4. *Was what he produced used successfully? If not, why not?*

B. Exercise in conducting an interview with a former manager.

Session II

I. OPENING REMARKS

A. Review of managers' experiences in interviewing.
B. Two major aspects of the interview.

1. *How to collect information about learning ability and motivation.*
2. *How to collect information about career aspirations.*

II. REVIEW OF SELECTION MADE

A. Manager's presentation of the selection made: name best candidate and defend position.
B. Two other managers discuss the presentation.
C. General discussion from the floor.
D. Suggestions for improvement.

III. THE JOB OFFER

A. Decisions to make

1. *Is candidate prepared to do the things you need done in your job?*
2. *Can the candidate learn what he needs to know within the time allotted to learning?*
3. *Is he willing to perform under your conditions?*

B. Clues to selling the job

1. *Career part of interview.*
2. *Your record or career matters.*
3. *Individual attention.*

IV. SUMMARY REMARKS

Companies that are the leaders in their respective fields in product, process, and technology are usually the leaders in the recruitment and development of superior professional, administrative, and managerial personnel. The selection workshop just outlined can help managers learn the kinds of questions to ask prospective candidates, recognize that it is as important to provide information as it is to get information, understand why candidates accept or turn down jobs and realize that it is important to question oneself before making a hiring decision.

The importance of selecting the right people is illustrated in the following example: A multimillion dollar company engaged in metal fabrication and machining had a once-in-a-lifetime opportunity to revise the incentive system for factory employees, eliminate such practices as banking parts for a rainy day and setting production limits, and gain control of operator down time. The new contract provided for the introduction of a standard-hour incentive plan. This had a potential for reducing labor costs by $300,000 over a three-year period. An outside consultant was called in to draw up a new incentive plan and was paid approximately $50,000 for his work.

To implement this new plan, a young, relatively inexperienced industrial engineer was hired at $10,000 a year to do a job which really required a $16,000 to $18,000 a year man. The vice-president of manufacturing made the wrong selection decision, for whatever reason. Two years later, the new incentive plan had not yet been implemented. Grievances increased, the program bogged down, and eventually both the industrial engineer and the vice-president of manufacturing were replaced.

So the manager with the open position to fill must ask himself, What is the exact assignment to be filled? What are the important qualifications, including experience, of the successful candidate? Better to take the time and spend the few extra dollars to find the right man. Other major considerations: Who are the people the new incumbent must deal with? What are their feelings and biases? Is the job properly structured, or is it set up organizationally in such a way that no one could succeed? How much aggressiveness should the new man have? And how much is too much or too little? Is he big enough for the job but not too big? How long is the man likely to remain with the company, and is it worth the calculated risk? Is he really the right man to fill a future key position?

To help in making this assessment, a manager has a right to find out whether the candidate's experience is directly related to the needs in depth, in quality, and in a comparable work environment. What kind of personalities has he dealt with? Has he dealt with them effectively? What are his strengths? His problem areas? What kinds of situations and people is he likely to have difficulty with? What are his intermediate and long-range career objectives? Why? How does he intend to achieve them? What accomplishments is he most proud of? What would he have done differently and why? An interview is good if the candidate talks at least 60 percent of the time and asks questions.

In talking with the prospective candidate, the manager should avoid asking questions which can be answered with a yes or no. Open-end questions are far preferable. Notes should not be taken during an interview. They make candidates uneasy and guarded in their responses. Periods of silence often mean discomfort, but a good interviewer can use silence to his advantage by getting the interviewee to elaborate on his answer.

Managers should know that the main reason why candidates accept or reject jobs is the nature of the work itself. If a candidate does not see the challenge or the opportunity, either it is nonexistent or the manager has failed to convey it properly. A work plan indicating expected results should be made available. Opportunities for advancement must be carefully defined. Earlier, it was noted that the job offer of the future will contain a plan for the candidate's career advancement along with the specifics of continuing his professional development.

In short, a job interview should reveal whether the interviewee has the aptitude, attitude, skills, abilities, experiences, education, personality, and so on that are required for satisfactory performance of the job.

When a selection workshop is utilized and the foregoing points are covered, improved results are achieved. For example, ten managers who had had a previous ratio of 1.5 acceptances to 5 offers in 40 contacts improved by setting a new record of 3.5 acceptances to 5 offers in 25 contacts after they attended a selection workshop. This was accompanied by a significant reduction in recruiting costs.

Leadership Skills

The quality of leadership manifests itself initially to the candidate in the selection process. Therefore, the manager's preparation may well decide whether he can manage his organization effectively.

Managers must earn and deserve the respect of their peers and subordinates as well as that of their superiors. Respect and acceptance of authority do not come automatically with a change in title. The manager does not *demand* intensity of work; he encourages, stimulates, and inspires. He expects his men to recommend decisions, ask questions, bring back wrong decisions for review and correction. His respect for his people is evident in his open-minded patience and tolerance for objections and differing opinions. He holds lively staff meetings every week. He consults his men before making plans or taking action which will affect them.

The effective leader is sensitive to and understands the individual's desires, objectives, feelings, ideas, and suggestions, and he tries to help make these consistent and consonant with organizational purposes. He teaches, coaches, advises, and counsels. While delegating responsibility and commensurate authority, he makes sure that his people's accomplishments are rewarded by recognition—tangible and intangible. He represents and supports the men who report to him. He knows how to resolve conflict—not by pretending it does not exist, nor by domination or force, but by finding new ways to integrate the best thinking of those in contention—through consultation.

The manager who does these things and does them well gets superior results because by challenging his people to do their best, by providing a vehicle such as management by objectives, he leads his people to new heights of achievement. Good leaders have few voluntary resignations and many promotions from within their groups. They develop their people and hence are more readily able to attract good people for continual infusion of new and creative talent.

The good leader personally insures that his new people are properly oriented and trained. He sets the stage for a good job of selection with a position description, a manpower specification, and a work plan for the first year. The manager fully communicates to the new employee his exact expectations, including his preferences and priorities for which goals need to be accomplished. He meets periodically with the new man to insure a good adjustment during those crucial early days. With the many pressures facing all managers, industrial socialization is not recognized as urgent and therefore is at least partially neglected. Yet the new employee must be properly and fully integrated into the team; it is necessary to obtain unity of purpose to achieve the most productive working climate.

Fundamentals of Good Control

The steps just outlined actually provide the best means of control because proper integration obviates the necessity for the more formal rigid controls. Controls are not meant to serve as a curb or restraint. Managers need to monitor the implementation of their plans, to follow up on their decisions, and to make adjustments as necessary. Any system of control must not only be simple; it must be adequate to the need and the situation; and it must be flexible, practical, timely. It should be tailor-made to feed back information the manager needs to make good decisions.

Controls help managers to manage their operations better by telling them where they have been, where they are, and where they are going. A management-by-objectives approach, it has been pointed out, provides built-in controls that enable a subordinate to monitor his own progress and seek assistance from his manager as needed. In this process, financial and accounting controls act as tools to tell an individual why, when, how, and what to do. Only when controls are used as restraints do they become self-defeating.

The human resources executive, with his knowledge of organization and manpower requirements, can assist general management in controlling the hiring of people to avoid excessive buildups which must inevitably end in cutbacks when business conditions deteriorate.

The effective manager has his staff participate in the establishment of controls to evaluate risks and minimize exposure on the downside while maximizing profit opportunity on the upside. One such technique for effective control is for a manager to query his staff on how best to control the unit's human resources to minimize or eliminate problems. The group should come to a meeting prepared to discuss human relations problems by priority of importance relative to their impact on costs, profits, innovation, growth, markets, quality, and delivery. The leader should list the problem areas, assign each a point value, and determine the group consensus. From this discussion and balloting, human relations goals could be developed to solve problems and take advantage of opportunities. Participation and involvement produce the best controls because they are based on voluntary acceptance and personal commitment.

Measurements and Feedback

Measuring the effectiveness of human resource management presents management's greatest challenge. Some new form of human asset accounting is needed to determine with some degree of precision how well a manager stacks up in this area of stewardship. Obviously, a net gain in human assets occurs with the hiring of a good manager; depletion occurs when one resigns.

Any action program worth planning is also worth measuring. Plans have no value unless they are implemented and realized. Assurance that performance is right for the situation requires that progress be measured at regular, predetermined intervals to compare actual progress with plan.

A manager cannot make good decisions about people if he does not have adequate, timely facts about the work situation. The task of measuring is complex, yet it is vital to do so as quantitatively as possible. The more a manager can measure, the more he can ask sound, balanced, objective, and persuasive questions. In this manner, he can make decisions that are clear and acceptable to all concerned.

The decentralization of managerial decision making mandates objective measurement of progress toward goals as contrasted with subjective appraisals and close personal supervision. In this way, attention can be focused on relevant issues and managing by exception, with an eye to future trends.

Measuring involves three steps. The first step is to devise and establish systems to evaluate all key areas where management attention is needed, to develop strengths while minimizing weaknesses, and to improve current and future human asset utilization. The second step is to analyze, appraise, and interpret results—in other words, to compare plans and performance against opportunities. This involves an analysis of deviation from standard. It involves making adequate information available to all concerned, in advance if possible, so reasoned decisions can be made on the basis of facts, not opinion. The third step is to make known the systems and the media and the results to all whose performance is measured so that this process of feedback will be used for continual individual and collective reappraisal and readjustment of the work and its performance.

Attitude Surveys

One good management tool for measuring the effectiveness of human resource utilization is the attitude survey, sometimes called the employee opinion or morale survey. It is in the form of a questionnaire designed to tell management about employee opinions and feelings on a variety of subjects dealing with human asset management. (A sample survey of employee attitudes is included in the Appendix.)

It also provides a measurement of the effectiveness of management's communication. Because it represents opinions, some of the findings may not appear to be entirely logical or justified from management's viewpoint. Nevertheless, a properly conducted survey does reveal what employees believe to be true. It reveals the facts as employees see them.

Because this is true, management, guided by the human resources executive, will find the information helpful in deciding what to do to improve morale, correct erroneous impressions, or alter the conditions that may be causing legitimate dissatisfactions. It should also indicate to management which of its employee relations policies and practices are on the right track in eliciting employee support.

These surveys are available commercially, and there are consultants who specialize almost exclusively in administration and interpretation of attitude surveys and follow-up of the findings.

Separate attitude surveys are administered to exempt, nonexempt salaried, and hourly employees. While 30 to 40 questions are included in each survey, the questions differ slightly for each group because the work requirements and conditions also differ.

When a company sponsors an attitude survey, it is saying to its employees: We need and want your ideas; we are interested in your point of view on matters that affect you. We need your cooperation to make our company stronger and a better place to work. Based on what you tell us, we will work with you to achieve the goals which evolve from the survey. Once the company has measured the level of employee morale, uncovered soft spots in the organization, found out what's on employees' minds, and determined the effectiveness of personnel programs, action is in order.

To achieve the best results, a good climate must be established for the survey. The atmosphere must be conducive to honesty and accuracy. To do this properly, the purpose and potential value of the survey must be communicated in advance to all employees; the need for cooperation and frank, honest answers must be stressed; the anonymity of the participants must be guaranteed; and the job must be done speedily and efficiently.

If these things are done well, managers will obtain first-hand information of how employees feel about their jobs, their bosses, their pay, their working conditions, their job relationships, the treatment they receive, and so on. A good survey provides data that serve as a reliable check on the accuracy and adequacy of information obtained through other sources and other measurements.

Some managers may voice strong opposition to attitude surveys—perhaps because they think they will be found wanting in their handling of people relationships or because they are fearful lest their inadequacies be revealed in the course of a survey. Yet the attitude survey really provides a tangible basis for assessing one of the most intangible aspects of management—the quality of its employee relations. It helps to give all employees a sense of participation; they see this as a means of getting through to top management.

In order to derive full benefits from the survey, the questionnaires should be given to groups of at least five employees each for purposes of identification. These work group results are the most meaningful because the variations in attitude from one group to the next are clearly differentiated, thus providing a basis for follow-up.

Complete reports should be made on top, middle, and lower management in areas of direct interest and concern to them so the findings can serve as a realistic springboard for planning future improvement in employee attitudes. Many of the implications of survey findings that are likely to elicit response and action at the lower levels of management might otherwise be ignored at the upper levels.

The human resources executive must make all data available to all personnel who have responsibility for employee relations activities. Survey results should be reported to all employees as soon as possible after the findings are tabulated. The report could be in the form of a specially printed booklet in addition to articles in the plant news and group informative meetings. This will show management's interest and desire to improve employee relations practices.

Authorities agree that there is little value in making a survey unless it is to be followed up. Follow-up is not easy. It involves more and better communication, and it takes time, but the results are more than worth the effort. Follow-up means that every manager and every supervisor must carefully study and analyze the findings as soon as possible after receiving them. Each must decide what remedial action is immediately practicable and feasible. He must tell his employees what the company plans to do and why. He must solicit their ideas. If action is not possible, he must explain why. Managers must either assign responsibility to follow up on survey findings or do it themselves. The thrust is toward prompt action and, as the action is taken, communication with employees about its relevance to survey findings. For maximum effectiveness, the survey should be repeated at the end of one year to measure improvement in job satisfaction.

Traditional Measurements Are Also Important

Earlier it was stated that employee relations practices are major causes of manifest problems such as low productivity, poor quality, missed delivery dates, and excessive costs. Personnel practices can be indirectly measured, for each manager, by the following standards:

- Turnover in terms of voluntary resignations.
- Attendance.

- Number of promotions made within the manager's operation and from his operation to other segments or functions of the enterprise.
- Number, frequency, and severity of lost-time accidents and dispensary visits involving hourly employees.
- Number and contributed value of ideas for improving operations which are submitted by hourly and salaried employees.
- Training time and loss of productivity to break in new employees.
- The existence or lack of formal orientation and indoctrination programs and regular follow-up meetings.
- Frequency of staff meetings.
- Use of management by objectives.
- The existence or absence of organization charts, position descriptions, and performance standards.
- The number, nature, and extent of expressed employee dissatisfactions at all levels.
- Difficulty or ease of recruitment of exempt employees—that is, the ratio of job offers to acceptances.
- What has been done to develop and improve the performance of key people.

A manager should be held fully accountable for the proper use and development of his human resources. These simple quantitative measures, coupled with the results of attitude survey findings, exit interviews, and counseling interviews by the human resources executive, will show how well or how poorly a manager is managing his human resources.

The Uses of Performance Appraisal

Measurement of performance encompasses appraisal of individuals and the collective work group as well as feeding back results to those appraised. Simply stated, performance appraisal is an attempt to think clearly about what each person does, how well he does it, and what his future prospects are when viewed against the background of his total work situation, including the direction and opportunities which his manager has provided.

The fact of the matter is that, whether the manager intends it or not, his every word, every suggestion, every criticism, every look tells a man how his performance is being judged. Each builds him up or tears him down. Performance appraisal is the most sensitive part of the manager's job. Either he uses this managerial tool effectively to build loyalty, teamwork, cooperation, and understanding or he abuses it and fails to achieve both highest job satisfaction and highest productivity. *All* employees have a right to be told where they stand, for better or for worse. The manner in which it is done is important.

What should a performance appraisal accomplish? This question was asked of 20 personnel directors who represented the composite opinion of 20 division presidents in a large decentralized company. The overwhelming majority cited a number of benefits to be derived from a well-administered performance appraisal system. The men had been brought together to consider the problems they faced in implementing such a system. During the day, four concurrent workshop sessions were held covering training and development, performance appraisal and salary administration, new employee orientation, and safety. The groups rotated. The memorandum in Exhibit 6-3 records the consensus of all four groups as to what performance appraisal should be and what it should do.

The groups further agreed that appraisal is a line responsibility, but specific guidelines are needed from the corporate office so that a factor such as a rating of outstanding in division A means the same thing as a rating of outstanding in division B—particularly where product, process, technology, and markets differ and the corporation is beginning to experiment with interdivisional promotional transfers.

The 20 personnel directors pointed out that feeding back results is perhaps the most important responsibility a manager has to his subordinates and to himself. How he handles this task will determine whether he builds or destroys morale, whether he increases or decreases productivity and profitability, and whether he helps or hinders individual development.

Feedback of results has many labels—performance appraisal, personnel evaluation, progress review, merit review, and a host of others. Whatever the label, there is much to be gained when a manager is conscientious about appraisal review. Formal appraisals serve a number of purposes. One of the most important is to pinpoint areas where improvement is needed. A second is to make clear who is responsible for what. A third is to reassess and communicate priorities. A fourth is to note obstacles so that they can subsequently be eliminated.

Performance appraisal should commend good work, serve as one base for pay increases and promotions, stimulate individual self-development, teach subordinates—and reveal how well a manager himself is doing and what some of his own developmental needs are.

Performance Standards

An appraisal session will be effective if a man's performance is evaluated against a set of standards which are understood by both

Exhibit 6-3.
CONSENSUS ON PERFORMANCE APPRAISAL

Memorandum to employee relations conference participants

The following reflects opinions and suggestions presented by the group on the subject of performance appraisals, specifically on four points: (1) what a performance appraisal should accomplish, (2) contents, (3) techniques of review, and (4) implementation.

1. What a performance appraisal should accomplish.
   a. Evaluate and measure a man's contribution.
   b. Do away with or at least reduce nepotism.
   c. Improve performance.
   d. Identify weaknesses and strengths.
   e. Help make good people available for promotion.
   f. Bridge the communication gap between a supervisor and his people.
   g. Provide guidelines for personal improvement.
   h. Help the manager to evaluate himself as a manager.
   i. Recognize and show appreciation for good work.
   j. Emphasize accomplishments instead of personality traits.
   k. Look to the future and set priorities and performance standards.
   l. Result in mutually agreed-upon goals for the ensuing year.
   m. Show a relationship between yearly performance and yearly salary.
2. Contents.
   a. Spell out what the man is responsible for.
   b. Show how more effective use can be made of the man's talents.
   c. Set priorities and performance standards.
   d. Set quantitative goals where possible.
   e. Be simple; be brief, confined to one or two pages.
   f. Provide for comments on the individual need for improvement.
3. Techniques.
   a. Both man and manager should prepare an appraisal on the man, then get together and compare notes.
   b. Focus on priorities and goals.
   c. Discussion should be a two-way street.
   d. Conduct the appraisal discussion in private.
   e. Give two-day notice of appraisal discussion.
   f. Conduct an appraisal at least once a year.
4. Implementation.
   a. Make performance appraisal a line responsibility; start at the top.
   b. Make it one of the manager's most important responsibilities.
   c. Have the personnel function develop guidelines; follow up.

The majority of the people in attendance felt that performance appraisal is necessary and can be of great use to the corporation as a talent bank. It is also of importance to the man, inasmuch as it gives him a way of communicating with his supervisor and sets forth a pattern of improvement.

parties. To put this in perspective we could call this process one of establishing performance budgets. At the beginning of each fiscal period, each man and his manager must set performance standards after thorough discussion and joint commitment.

The human resources executive can suggest a technique wherein the manager describes on paper the conditions that should exist at the end of the period if the man performs his duties to the manager's satisfaction. The man, in turn, should go through the same process, recording his concept of the conditions that should exist if he carries out his responsibilities to the satisfaction of his manager.

The final document, as in the management-by-objectives approach described in Chapter 5, clearly identifies the areas for which the man is personally accountable along with an objective for each where appropriate. The end results are then described in terms of the conditions that should exist at the end of the appraisal period. This approach should require the man to spell out in advance exactly what must be done, by whom, and when in order to advance the objective. He must be prepared to describe how the work will be divided and accomplished and the results when the work is done. Time taken in this phase, particularly by the manager in doing this with each of his key people and in interrelating their goals, will save countless hours of floundering around during the fiscal year. If possible, these statements of results should be limited to the six or eight major problem and opportunity areas.

The goals should be stated quantitatively whenever possible, and progress should really be reviewed monthly—particularly for new employees who are not yet prepared to take the initiative in this process. It is preferable that each man submit a brief monthly report commenting on his progress toward achievement of his goals. These monthly reports should discuss deviations from standard and identify the conditions affecting achievement. If a good job has been done on setting standards and monitoring progress, the stage is set for a constructive discussion.

The form that best meets the criteria of the 20 personnel directors is illustrated in Exhibit 6-4.

Conducting the Appraisal Discussion

A number of interesting on-the-job studies indicate that more productive and constructive man–manager appraisal discussions result from the use of a performance appraisal form prepared by the subordinate as contrasted with the usual form prepared by the manager.

Exhibit 6-4.

QUANTITATIVE PERFORMANCE STANDARDS

Personnel Evaluation

Date of Appraisal 4/1/—

Individual Appraised
Name: Peter Charles
Birth date: 1/9/29
Title: Plant Manager
Div.: Elite Press Company
Date started present job: Jan. '65
Date started with company: Feb. '59

Individual's manager: John Amos
Title: VP, Manufacturing
How long have you been his manager? Jan. '65
How long have you known appraisee? Mar. '55
In what relationship?
He was my Production Control Manager from 1955–1959

Manager's Concept of 6–8 Major Responsibilities of the Appraisee's Position:	Performance Commentary:
1. Hold production to 98% of schedule	1. Met 90% of schedule
2. Hold rejects to 2% of total production	2. Rejects were 5% of total production
3. Build effective, cohesive production team by 2/1/—	3. Selection good but coordination of effort lacking
4. Reduce inventory investment by $100,000 from 19—	4. 19— average inventory reduced by $45,000 at same volume
5. Reduce machine down time from 8% to 3%	5. Machine down time reduced to 5%
6. Reduce manufacturing variances from 8% to 2%	6. Reduced manufacturing variances to 3%
7. No lost time because of labor problems	7. Four grievances resolved; need to control union time
8. Submit all required production and variance reports on time	8. Submitted three reports late; one had questionable figures

Factors Affecting Job Performance

X Ability to withstand pressure
X Job knowledge
__ Work accomplishment
X Quality
O Measuring/self-appraisal
O Communicating skills
O Planning skills
__ Managerial ability
__ Initiative
__ Analytical ability

Place "X" in front of 3 factors in which person is strongest.
Place "O" in front of 3 factors in which most improvement needed.

3–5 Strongest Job-Related Assets and How Demonstrated:

1. Excellent grasp of new production control system.
2. Strong quality control program, particularly in final inspection.
3. Knows shop, equipment, and people inside out.
4. Works well under pressure.
5. Maintains excellent labor relations.

3–5 Strongest Job-Related Limitations and How Noted:

1. Needs to plan manpower more effectively.
2. Needs closer control over plant operations.
3. Lost time in transfer of products from operation to operation.
4. Needs to develop in-depth knowledge of cost system and controls.

Performance on Present Job
1 2 (3+) 4 5

Promotability Rating
A (B) C D E

To what positions and when?
Vice-President–Manufacturing in 2–3 years

Developmental Needs:

1. Attend outside school at least twice annually, 6 to 12 weeks a year.
2. Become active in a professional organization.
3. Head up a cost improvement task force.
4. Start a reading program in modern management practices and techniques.

Additional Comments
Health is excellent
Attitude is excellent

Manager's Signature Date: 4/2/—
Review Acknowledged Date: 4/2/—
Manager's Manager: Sam Haines, Pres. Date: 4/4/—
Copies: Manager, Executive Development

One such study by a large electrical manufacturer was carried out under carefully controlled conditions and followed up. Managers found out that self-appraisal was especially effective with marginal performers. In the experimental or pilot group, a superior upward flow of information resulted, and managers learned how employees perceived their job responsibilities, their performance, and the problems they encountered. When a man has to quantify and review his own performance, he seems to get a clearer perception of his job duties and the causes of underachievement and to form a more realistic picture of his own performance.

Differences of opinion are often resolved or at least clarified when man and manager talk about where and how they differ in their perceptions of expectations and results. Frequent discussions of issues, problems, and results do contribute to high employee morale and the development of constructive man–manager relationships. When the employee feels that he is really doing important work, his production will improve along with his morale. A majority of managers prefer having the subordinate prepare an appraisal. Some favor having both man and manager fill out a form in pencil, exchange copies in draft form, and hold a constructive discussion. In future sessions, performance is less likely to fall short of expectations following a discussion that is based on the subordinate's self-appraisal.

This study revealed that, while the most beneficial effects were on low-rated employees, the best employee reaction came from subordinates who had had no previous appraisal discussions with their managers. Employees with a high need for independence reacted very favorably to the use of self-appraisal. Ratings were more realistic with this approach than with the traditional manager-prepared form.

It seems clear that the employee must be a full participant both in setting standards and in evaluating and discussing results. Regardless of format used, a number of techniques seem to generate superior results in terms of attaining full benefit from the actual discussion with the employee. Managers should be aware that a number of factors will affect individual receptivity. Some of these factors are age, experience, rivalries, on-the-job and off-the-job pressures, length of time on this assignment, his desire for advancement and recognition, and the extent to which these desires have been met in the past.

Manpower Reviews

With a good performance review behind him, each manager should be prepared to discuss his manpower situation in an annual manpower review. The human resources executive should lead this review, which should be separate from annual profit plan or financial reviews. This is exclusively a human resources review. The chief policy makers and appropriate group executives should participate in this discussion.

A manpower review is designed to improve a manager's understanding of his subordinates' present and potential performance so he can make better promotion decisions that are based on more realistic manpower planning and utilization.

Manpower reviews conclusively demonstrate top management interest in the development of people. Managers should be asked to be thoroughly prepared for these reviews; meetings should be scheduled three months in advance. In their preparation, serious replacement problems will be highlighted in advance. A more critical look will be taken at poor performers as managers prepare a plan for action on manpower problems. The fact that an entire meeting is focused on management manpower resources will help to counteract the tendency to delay decisions and action about people because of work pressures. And finally, a sound basis is provided for manpower development because people with high potential become known to the most senior members of the management team.

This is the procedure. At least three months ahead of the scheduled meeting, each key manager who will be expected to review his people is sent a list of questions to be discussed. He is also asked to bring to this meeting copies of his organization chart as one of the bases for his review. It should be noted that these reviews are best conducted in an informal atmosphere; structured presentations should be discouraged. But each manager is expected to define his plans to capitalize on his strengths and correct his weaknesses, organizationally speaking. The discussion should consider managers, supervisors, and key specialists.

While informality is encouraged, each manager must demonstrate that he really knows his people by covering the following ground:

- The performance of each key man in terms of managerial, technical, and professional results, including the development of his own people where appropriate.
- What he himself has done in the past year to improve the performance of his key people and the extent to which his annual review helped, if at all.
- What specifically he plans to do, including timing, to handle less than satisfactory performance.
- What are his most likely replacement needs over the next two years? Who are the most likely internal candidates? What is he

doing to get them ready? Where no internal candidates are available, what are his recruitment plans?

- What are some of the more significant things the managers who report to him are doing to improve the performance and promotability of their key people?
- Who are his own immediate, near-term (two to three year), and long-term (three to ten year) executive backups?
- How many unsatisfactory performers has he removed from their jobs during the year? Where did they go?
- Who are his five weakest and his five strongest performers, and what is he doing and planning to do for each?
- What has he done about establishing personnel development goals at all levels of his organization, and how has he communicated this to get maximum benefit?
- What has been his experience in delegation—successful or otherwise? How does he plan to improve his delegation of responsibility, authority, and accountability?
- What has he done to improve the working climate in his operations, and what effects have his actions had on motivation?
- What problems has he detected in integrating the work of his operations with that of others?
- How does he tell his people about areas requiring managerial attention, and what are some examples of results?
- What has been his progress in recruiting and developing minority group executives?

A manager who has to prepare himself for this kind of review will surely come to know all his key people better; he will communicate more with them and he will spur their own self-development efforts.

What to Do with the Marginal Employee

With all the recent emphasis on identification and development of the superior performer, the literature has all but neglected an equally difficult and more troublesome problem—marginal performance.

Performance is marginal when it is near or at the lower limit of acceptability. This determination is made by his immediate manager. Every employee must be given the opportunity to demonstrate whether he can make the expected contribution. His immediate manager is responsible for insuring that this opportunity has been provided.

The human resources executive must provide guidelines for handling problems of marginality, including early discovery, so that managers can attain the most effective utilization of manpower in meeting business objectives.

The manager's judgment should be based on a sound evaluation of the individual's contribution to business objectives through measurement of actual results against predetermined standards of performance for the position. Measurements should be sufficiently revealing to identify minimum acceptable work over a sustained period. Marginal does not mean unqualified or incompetent. It does not mean absolute failure to achieve goals, whether because of inability or unwillingness. Out-and-out failure calls for prompt termination.

Obviously, persons new to their positions and trainees who have potential are *not* considered to be marginal performers.

Marginality, like obsolescence, is no respecter of titles or organizational levels; it can be found at any level of the organization among relatively short-service employees, seasoned employees, newly transferred employees, newly promoted employees, and longer-service employees.

The marginal employee may really be trying to do a good job. Conceivably, he lacks capacity, ability, education, or appropriate experience. He may suffer from physical or emotional problems, or he may have lost interest because of a personality conflict or organizational change. The individual whose work is marginal on his present assignment may be helped to improve his performance by his manager. Each situation must be handled individually.

A good performance appraisal system should identify signs of marginality early. The results-oriented appraisal, quantified where possible, will readily uncover areas of underachievement or individual lack of effectiveness. Usually, six months to a year is plenty of time to recognize and turn around marginal performance. Prompt action is necessary for a number of reasons. For example, the judgments, decisions, and actions of exempt employees have a great deal of impact, good or bad, on the total organization. This is particularly true at the higher organizational levels. Moving in quickly will contribute to the attainment of improved results.

As part of the manpower review, at least as much attention should be directed toward the least effective performers as is directed toward the superior performers. The intent is to make sure that appropriate action is taken, but to avoid overconcentration on poor performers. Balanced attention is necessary.

The manager must review the marginal contributor's total work history; he must evaluate the employee's net worth as a potential contributor to the success of the business. Here, the help of the human resources executive in putting together a dossier can prove valuable.

After determining the present and possible future compatibility of the individual with present and future business needs, the manager should review his findings with *his* manager. At this point, the course of action may involve retention on the present job, transfer, or termination. The preferred solution is to so improve the individual's performance that retention or transfer becomes the most appropriate action. Retention will require coaching and guidance for a reasonable time to permit the marginal employee to improve his performance against specific plans, standards, and measures. The individual must clearly understand what constitutes success or failure in the event of a transfer or retention on his present job.

It is a wise investment in human resources if an experienced individual who has in the past demonstrated good capability can be utilized in a capacity appropriate to his personal needs and consonant with business needs. His adjustment to his new circumstances, particularly in a downgrade, must be carefully assessed in determining an appropriate course of action.

Where termination appears to be the best solution, the real reasons must be clearly documented as a matter of precaution. If optional retirement, appropriate separation allowance, or other considerations are possible, a voluntary acceptance by the individual is preferable. Discharge should be the last resort.

Every manager must resolve his problems of employee ineffectiveness; this will help to provide for continuing achievement in upgrading the performance of the entire workforce. Timely accomplishment and follow-up in these situations is a gauge of the manager's ability. The role of the human resources executive is to provide policy guidelines, procedures, and proper systems of appraisal and development as well as expert counseling and advice to the managers involved.

7
Organizational Climate: Stimulant or Depressant

The development of an organization structure which can create, adapt to, and prosper with change represents a major challenge to the human resources executive and the chief executive officer.

The problem is not one of developing appropriate objectives; most companies do this reasonably well, and a number of examples have been presented. The problem seems to revolve around the development of an organization design to meet these objectives. More is involved here than merely shuffling titles from block to block on paper or following the principles described in the preceding chapter. This is not to minimize their importance, because they are necessary. But the manager is dealing with *human* resources and with variations in individual availability, competence, personality, and goals. He must organize these into a logical structure that most effectively utilizes each key individual's knowledge, talents, and energy. Thus building the organization structure is fundamental to building a smoothly functioning team in an organizational environment that stimulates and motivates rather than stifles or depresses.

Too often people do not fully understand the objectives they must meet and hence do not identify with them. An audit or evaluation of the effectiveness of an organization must recognize the importance of people's reaction to it. No organization can afford a structure or climate that makes less than full use of the potential of its human resources. The good executive perceives this and persistently seeks to improve the organization structure and the operating relationships which promote a healthy organizational climate for growth and development.

In many small and medium companies and a few large ones the existent organization structure is the result of an evolutionary process and bears little relationship to the strategies or management needs of the company. An organization structure, like a manager, can become obsolete by failing to keep pace with the changing times.

While mere recognition of a need to change an organization structure will not in itself produce the change, a clear delineation of signs suggesting a need to change may awaken sufficient response to minimize intimidation by conservative managers and force a consideration of what is required to operate profitably and insure future growth.

A number of indicators suggest opportunities to build a climate of organizational stimulation through change. For example, major executive changes because of retirements, deaths, resignations, or new hires may be just the thing to create a climate for change. If a company is in a period of major expansion or retrenchment, if it is acquiring or divesting product lines or properties, if it experiences a significant change in volume—up or down—the human resources executive has another excellent opportunity to bring about major organizational improvement in cooperation with senior line managers.

In our present environment of continually accelerating technological change, the products themselves as well as the processes and equipment required to produce them are caught up in this trend. As the needs for change are perceived, the human resources executive can pay some attention to human engineering as well as organizational improvement. Given adequate planning, changes can have a decided plus value in organizational relationships. This was illustrated by a general manager of a large appliance manufacturer who was planning to make a number of key executive realignments in conjunction with the introduction of the new line. Before any press releases were given out, he called all the plant population together (on company time) and personally introduced the new executives; announced the realignment of responsibility; and had each of his key managers discuss the new products and their role in the manufacture, sale, and distribution of the line. The response was tremendous; there was complete acceptance of the need for change and the employees' role in implementing changes.

Top managers are rapidly being conditioned to respond to changes in their external environment, whether legislative, economic, or social. How much better if, through the human resources executive, they would anticipate these changes and prepare their businesses (and hence their organizations and people) to take advantage of the opportunities offered by these forces for improving organizational climate—instead of merely reacting in traditional fashion.

Frequently, top line executives evidence some interest in providing avenues of advancement to accelerate the growth of young people with high potential. This can be accomplished by using certain positions for developmental purposes—for example, the administrative assistant, or the manager of executive development, or the management-by-objectives coordinator. Another key position for accelerated advancement would be the business planner. These attempts are usually successful and help to improve morale if superior people are brought in, identified early in their careers, and given really responsible assignments with commensurate authority.

Often an organization shows unmistakable signs of a need to reorganize and hence improve its internal climate and efficiency. One of the first signs is a slowness in decision making or execution. When things bog down, and no one seems to know why, there is more often than not an organizational deficiency. Slowness in decision making is frequently accompanied by serious errors. One example of this was the purchase by a company president of an invention (a rubber-molding press) to fabricate rubber. Two prototypes were built, the product was manufactured and offered for sale, and then it was discovered—too late—that the market was seriously limited, and the product was soon dropped from the line. No market study had been made prior to the purchase of patent rights. Engineers working on the product became discouraged, and the organization climate went sour.

In like vein, shipping too much or too little of an order or shipping the wrong order can wreak havoc in the shipping, sales, order service, and manufacturing departments. Mistakes like these point to inadequacies in people or organization; and in either event, the loss of customers makes for a stifling organization climate.

Inadequate or ineffective communication, production bottlenecks, lagging paperwork, and missed schedules are symptomatic of a tired organizational climate lacking in vitality. Executive performance drops below par when personal goals are not identified with company goals. High absenteeism and turnover rates are indicative of a tired climate.

When executives are overworked and suffering through a 70- to 80-hour week, either there is an insufficient number of good executives to do the job, or the executives do not know what to do; they work too hard and accomplish little.

Where managers, supervisors, and subordinates continue to do the same things in the same way year after year and new ideas are clearly lacking, where there is little or no long-range planning, the organizational climate is poor and dry rot is setting in.

An organization should not be considered healthy only when things are running smoothly, without friction or strong difference of opinion. On the other hand, a hard look needs to be taken where there are staff–line conflicts, interdepartmental frictions, or personality clashes. Conflict can be very useful to building a healthy organizational climate if it brings together different points of view to identify relevant alternatives for the decision makers. It is particularly important in a new or rapidly changing organization that conflicts not be buried or completely resolved at lower levels. Top management can be shut off from its vital communication lifeline if conflict is suppressed. This is also important because, when disagreements are pinpointed, top management can clarify issues and serve up policies to guide others faced with similar situations and problems.

When conflicts arise from personality differences, jurisdictional status, or confused assignments or responsibility, they are harmful, tend to divide the staff, and lead to antagonisms, all of which stifle organizational spirit and drive. In contrast, the proper organizational climate helps to build loyalty by welcoming and rewarding new ideas and by promoting problem-solving rather than precedent-following solutions.

A mature organization does not suffer from poor control, missing information, partial knowledge of results, or failures through inefficient committee work, imbalance, unclear objectives, or excessive use of control. A well-managed situation has simple feedback mechanisms to keep in control. People want to work for a well-run organization and not for a loser. The successful company owes its success in some degree to having built a stable but flexible organization and a climate of constructive positive attitudes.

When Should Organizational Changes Be Made?

The timing of major shifts or realignments in the structure depends to a large degree on the urgency of the situation. For example, if a company has had the inventory control staff reporting to the sales department for several years, in all probability an immediate change would not significantly affect the profit and loss statement. If problems are being experienced, a reorganization per se will not solve all the problems. Any major change can create new problems while solving old ones. The timing will depend to some degree on the level of morale. Couple this with the degree to which employees have been accustomed to accept change through preconditioning and you get some idea as to how rapidly you can proceed.

The company that believes in participation can effect change more rapidly because it has previously involved its people in change, and it can more readily implement a major shift in organization or business strategy without negative effect on morale.

Timing of organizational changes is dependent to some extent on the ease with which new systems and procedures can be adopted and assimilated into the fabric of the formal organization. Naturally, the more the preconditioning and the greater the number and frequency and impact of previous changes, the greater the receptivity of those affected by the change and hence the better the organizational climate.

The readiness of people to accept organizational change will also affect the timing of a change. For example, if the present organization is top-heavy and therefore hurting the company economically and psychologically, employees will be receptive to change, even if a number of them are affected by it. A turnover of key executives coincident with major change is generally accepted in times of dire adversity with relatively little resistance. There *are* times when conditions and people are ripe for a change. Proper communication of a change, in advance, can stimulate a favorable reaction and can at the same time improve the organizational climate. It is usually obvious to everybody when the belt needs to be tightened.

From a top management viewpoint, when there is poor control, slow or inadequate communication of results, poor compliance, and too much dispersion of responsibility through ineffective committees, it is time for a good hard look at the present organization structure and climate along with the effects that each has on motivation and productivity.

Just a thorough, careful scrutiny of the organization chart may yield clues to cost improvement and organizational climate improvement. The formal organization chart can and should be audited. It should be constructed from information gleaned from a number of sources to determine who really reports to whom. Specifically, existing records should be examined, including announcements from the chief executive and orders from management. A close look should be directed at procedures and job descriptions. Job descriptions should be prepared where there are none, and they should indicate where each position reports as well as all the positions that report to it. These should be sketched out by functions and by reporting relationships. Decision-making authority needs to be reviewed and factored in. The work flow, lines of communication, and key document distribution routes need to be followed. This information can be secured by interview and questionnaire.

While a sustained investment in human resources should be encouraged, this does not mean permitting the situation to get out of hand. Each trainee should earn his salary through productive, profitable work. Having too many trainees is as bad as having too few. They expect rapid advancement to positions of increasing responsibility. Failure to provide this insures a high turnover rate.

There may be too many layers of management. Besides making communication more difficult, this situation requires excessive coordination and promotes inefficiency. Certain functions may be reporting too high in the organization. As an example, a metal fabricating company has a vice president of purchasing who reports to the president. Materials costs represent about 55 percent of total manufacturing costs, and most items purchased with a high dollar value are standard shelf items of vendors. Here is a clear example of a man who does not belong in the business policy group. He is overcompensated, and he should report to the vice-president of manufacturing, who is rightly a member of the business policy group.

A man's title and staff may be disproportionate to the size and needs of the business, thus incurring needlessly excessive costs. Poor control over titles also leads to confusion. Wherever possible, staffing ratios should be compared to those of competitors. Staffing could be unreasonable even in a profitable company. One way to check out the measured value of each position is to determine as precisely as possible its contribution to business results. Some positions—coordinator, assistant-to, liaison—will almost automatically eliminate themselves.

The foregoing examples of organizational shortcomings bring about a depressing organizational climate. Employees know when there is an awkward, cumbersome arrangement—sometimes accommodative in nature—that contributes to buck-passing and delays. A vibrant, healthy organization that stimulates and motivates is neither overweight nor underweight; it does not bulge out at the sides or stretch disproportionately upward or downward.

In ascertaining whether an organization shows signs of sickness or health, the human resources executive should review with the chief line executive whether specific provision has been made for the management of all essential activities. In the process, the two should ascertain whether any functions have been assigned to more than one unit in the organization.

It is quite possible in a rapidly growing company that the responsibilities of one or more key people have become too numerous and too complex to be handled effectively. In that event, the jobs should be split into logical elements for better control. In the long run it may be far less expensive to have two people take over a job now being done by one man.

Provision must be made for the clear written definition of responsibility, authority, and accountability for each executive position at a minimum. This is not automatically understood or properly implemented in many companies. Not all managers know whom they report to or are sure who reports to them. Sometime managers report to three or four bosses. This cannot possibly promote organizational harmony and a strong esprit de corps.

Some managers forget there is an organization structure in dealing with subordinates. While this can be justifiable in rare situations of expediency or emergency, it is an undesirable habit to get into because it undermines the authority and reduces the effectiveness of subordinate managers. In one such situation, the chief union representative made it a point to visit the company president with a grievance. The president promptly resolved the grievance in the union's favor without checking first with the foreman, superintendent, or industrial relations manager. That company ended up with more than a thousand formal, written, unresolved grievances because the chief executive bypassed the formal lines of authority. And this single act virtually destroyed the morale of the first-line supervisors. Top executives must exercise control through attention to policy matters and problems of exceptional importance rather than through review of or interference with routine matters.

Defining and measuring organizational climate can be an elusive exercise. If management recognizes that there is competition between companies at the level of creative innovation in all business functions, it will program for and properly manage change in order to stay on top. Organizations must create changes in their environment and not merely adapt to them under pressure.

The very first requirement in overcoming obstacles to successful management of change is a determination to grow. Given this determination, management will recognize the price that must be paid and will willingly commit funds for growth. If top management establishes a climate of growth and encourages lower-level managers to develop, innovate, and expand their thinking, the company will grow instead of being content with routine day-to-day administration and improvements in operating efficiency. To translate thinking into action requires planning and may require a full-time business planner. The organization must constantly reshape its objectives and work at building a favorable attitudinal climate for growth and change.

The organization's attention to its external environment must be strong and systematic. Too often organizations devote a disproportionate amount of time to an analysis of what goes on inside the company. Organizational climate is not built entirely on internal factors, but is significantly affected by the external environment—competition, growth opportunities, distribution patterns, transportation costs, legislation, technological trends, changing customer requirements, socioeconomic changes. Paying close attention to these factors poises an organization for movement when the time becomes ripe. It stimulates internal climate improvement and pride in a forward-thinking company.

Once plans are devised to deal with major issues and major opportunities in the external environment they must be implemented. This may require pooling of talent and providing for necessary checks and balances. Information organization and flow must be developed. It may be necessary for tomorrow's business manager to completely restructure and reshape his organization to cope with modern society. This takes a great deal of courage and capacity. It takes superior people who must be developed over a period of years. Good organizational climate does not come about by accident; it is the result of good planning and careful implementation.

Internal Factors in Assessing Organizational Climate

To manage change successfully, a company must mobilize its total internal resources, human and material, in pursuit of carefully defined objectives—which should obviously include human resource objectives.

An organization can be thought of as having a personality of its own. That is to say, it possesses a certain combination of characteristics which make it healthy or sick, growing or stagnant, vibrant or tired, autocratic or democratic, motivational or stifling. Therefore, it is important to examine those internal factors which contribute to positive or negative climate, to a stimulating or a depressing environment.

One such factor is the nature of the leadership processes used by the executives and managers, starting with the chief decision makers. It might be interesting to rate all these factors as they are discussed on a one-to-three scale to assess the organization climate in your company: (1) excellent; (2) reasonably satisfactory; (3) poor or marginal and in need of major improvement.

The first characteristic in the leadership process is the degree to which managers demonstrate trust and confidence in their subordinates by delegating to them full authority, control, and accountability for making decisions on matters of importance. The values in this characteristic range from complete trust and confidence (1) to limited trust with reservation (2) to a lack of trust and confidence (3).

A closely related characteristic is the subordinates' willingness to come in of their own accord and freely discuss job-related matters with their managers. In many situations the so-called open-door policy is given only lip service. The manager's attitude, behavior, and receptivity actually discourage all comers from entering his theoretically open door. The best situation is one in which there is a regular flow of traffic to the manager's office initiated by subordinates to review matters of importance and communicate problems and opportunities (rated 1). In a different situation a subordinate does come in occasionally, but speaks guardedly because of his concern for the boss's reaction (this is rated 2). In yet another situation subordinates deliberately sweep problems under the rug, screen out information, and impede the flow of communication (this is rated 3). The last of these situations means that the manager's past behavior and attitude have been such that the subordinates fear a punitive or negative reaction so much that they prefer to take their chances by withholding information.

On the other hand, it is equally important to evaluate the manager's success in getting from his subordinates new, constructive, innovative ideas for improving operations. The best manager (rated 1) easily obtains ideas and generally makes constructive use of them—or at least tries to. If the ideas come in with little regularity and the manager occasionally makes some effort to use them, he receives a value of 2. The manager who rarely gets voluntarily submitted ideas for improvement and seldom uses them when he does get them receives a value of 3.

The leadership process has a direct effect on the attitudes people develop toward the organization and toward its goals. If most of the ratings fall in the first category, people's attitudes can be expected to be highly favorable, and consequently their behavior will be directed toward implementing organizational goals. If the ratings come closer to an average of 3, it can be expected that hostile attitudes exist or are developing, and people's behavior will run counter to the goals of the organization.

The nature of the communication process is also a highly significant factor in influencing organizational climate. For example, if the information flow is upward, downward, and across, and if the information itself is generally accepted in all directions or at least openly and candidly reviewed and discussed, a value of 1 should be assigned. If part is accepted and part is viewed with suspicion (up or down), or if the boss gets only good news or filtered news, a value of 2 should be assigned. If information at most levels is viewed with great suspicion and tends to be inaccurate, a value of 3 should be assigned.

Teamwork is another factor with a great deal of influence on organizational climate. If there is obviously a substantial amount of cooperation throughout the organization, even among people at different levels who are not in a direct reporting relationship, this interaction should be rated 1—excellent. If, however, there is limited interaction among individuals and groups at different levels, and group interaction is approached with caution, a value of 2 should be assigned. If there is very little interaction among organization levels, a distinct lack of teamwork, and an aura of fear and distrust, a value of 3 should be assigned.

Who makes the decisions, and where, is another significant variable affecting organizational climate for better or for worse. If decision making is characterized by group participation, involvement, and usually consensus, and if the people are generally aware of the problems (particularly at the lower levels), a value of 1 should be assigned. If the superiors usually make the decisions, but discuss the problems with their people and know of the problems within the groups, a value of 2 should be assigned. When a superior makes his own decisions without discussing them with or involving his people and is often only partially aware of lower-level problems, a value of 3 should be assigned.

Decision making can contribute little or nothing toward motivating people to implement the decisions, or it can make a substantial contribution toward motivating people to accept and act on decisions. The same considerations are true in goal setting. Goals have an excellent chance of being accepted if people participate in setting them. But if a manager merely issues orders (usually in memo form with little explanation) goals will be resisted even though acceptance may be indicated.

The manner in which performance is controlled is another characteristic with a high degree of impact on organizational climate. If the concern for control permeates the entire organization, if there is control and review at lower as well as higher levels, and if controls are not used as restraints but as management tools for self-guidance and coordinated problem solving, a 1 rating should be assigned.

If there is some downward delegation of review and control, and if lower and higher levels of management use controls for some policing with emphasis on reward more than on punishment, a value of 2 should be assigned. Where controls are highly concentrated at the top management level for the most part and are used primarily for policing and primarily for meting out punishment for failure to meet performance standards, a value of 3 should be assigned.

The foregoing scale of ratings can be used in a variety of ways by the manager who seeks to improve his organizational climate. He can, for example, analyze and rate his own operation as he sees it. Then he can ask all his subordinates to do likewise, promising them immunity and insuring anonymity. The comparison of the manager's ratings with those of his people may be revealing. In an event, some areas for improvement will be identified. Just as in the attitude survey. these should be communicated, and definite plans for improvement should be developed and implemented. It would be ideal if all managers and all subordinates participated in this evaluation of organization climate and the results were identified by organization level and by work group within each level.

The Organizational Profile

Another interesting exercise which senior and junior managers can participate in with the guidance of the human resources executive is to meet together in an effort to identify the positive elements in the organization that contribute to the realization of organizational goals as well as the negative elements that represent barriers to improved performance. Since these impressions should represent individual ideas, the format in Exhibit 7-1 should be completed by all managers.

During the meeting work groups should be set up, each with a chairman, democratically elected by secret ballot, as well as a recorder (also elected). Members of the group should be given one hour to complete the profile in Exhibit 7-1 and asked to reassemble. The chairman should then summarize the profiles and serve as team spokesman when the consensus of the group is reported to top management.

A variation for managers interested in improving the organizational climate would be to repeat this same exercise, but ask each member of the group to identify present and future characteristics, internal and external, which could affect company growth, prosperity, human resource management, and so on. Alongside each characteristic identified, the participant should note what he thinks the company is doing about it now and should do in the future.

A final variation might be to ask each participant in the exercises to spell out the implications of his assessments as to what will be required of managers in the future in terms of knowledge, experience,

Exhibit 7-1.
ORGANIZATIONAL PROFILE ASSESSMENT

Positive elements	Reasons for them	Action to emphasize
________	________	________
________	________	________
Negative elements	**Reasons for them**	**Action to minimize**
________	________	________
________	________	________

attitudes, interests, and abilities and to have them note what they feel the company is doing now as against what it should be doing and when. A great deal can be accomplished through these approaches in a one- to two-day session on assessment and improvement of organization climate.

The reports obviously are not intended to be an academic exercise or to gather dust on the shelf. They are intended rather to be used in summary form as a basis for top-level policy discussion and formulation by the business policy group.

The Annual Management Meeting

One of the greatest opportunities for improving the organizational climate is the annual management meeting. Yet such a meeting may fail to take full advantage of this opportunity for several reasons, including the following: The facility is not carefully chosen; the wrong people or not enough of the right people are invited; the sessions are too long or too short; the objectives are poorly defined; there is a lack of participation and involvement; communication is from the top down; too much attention is focused on problem solving and dwelling on past mistakes instead of looking ahead to future opportunities; too much or too little time is spent on recreation; major priorities are not clearly identified because there is no theme to focus on; insufficient time is allowed for planning the meeting; too few people do too little homework; the meeting is not evaluated, so there is little improvement from one year to the next; there is no follow-up to reach those who did not attend.

While this section is not intended to be a treatise on how to plan, run, control, and follow up on a management meeting, the key points that spell the difference between a resounding success—calling forth rededication and enthusiasm—and a mediocre meeting that has no significant effect are worthy of mention.

To emphasize the positive, a good meeting will be described in detail in the following pages. The meeting was held by a large U.S. conglomerate that has 20 decentralized divisions operating as separate profit centers with sales, manufacturing, control, and personnel responsibilities. But first, some guidelines.

Top Management Participation

A management meeting is the president's meeting, so he should be heavily involved in the planning, implementation, participation, and follow-up. The following guides are not listed in order of importance, except in a general way.

Who makes the arrangements: *one man or a committee?* In a busy organization, there is generally no one of sufficient stature who can devote full time for two or three months to planning and preparations for such a meeting. Accordingly, a temporary committee of two or three well-regarded staff and line executives should be appointed to take responsibility for the meeting. Generally, the human resources executive should chair the committee since he assumes a major role in its success. Others who might be involved are the corporate planner, an administrative staff vice-president, and a high-ranking line executive. The president should personally appoint these people and meet with them to stress the importance he places in this meeting.

Selecting the site and the participants. The site selection should be based on an estimate of the number who will attend. Depending on location, three to six months' advance reservation time is mandated, particularly for a large group. In the meeting described, approximately 140 attended, including directors, all corporate officers, group executives, key staff personnel, and, from each of the 20 divisions, the president and his chief manufacturing, marketing, engineering, and financial executives. The personnel director should of course be among the key staff personnel in attendance.

Among the major factors in site selection are the guarantee of sufficient good single rooms for everybody in attendance (to insure this, a personal visit for inspection is a must), quality of food and service, accessibility by public transportation, probable weather conditions, and costs. There are organizations that specialize in helping managers to select appropriate meeting sites; using such an organization is one way to insure adequacy of meeting rooms, equipment, and so on.

The theme sets the tone. Whether in times of adversity or in times of prosperity, the theme is highly important because it sets the mood and attitude of the participants. The theme selected on this particular occasion was intended to deal with a current period of adversity with its mood of austerity: Maintaining profits was extremely difficult, costs were rising while the line was being held on prices, there were fewer people to do more work, sales were down, and morale was suffering in the face of a shrinking bonus.

Against this backdrop of gloom and pessimism, the task was to report on the past, gird belts, and prepare to build for the future. The theme was "Business fundamentals—Our way of life." The group of senior officers enthusiastically accepted and supported this theme because it seemed to meet their objectives, present and future.

Objectives of the meeting. There were six objectives: to provide for

(1) improved communication from the top down and from the bottom up; (2) cross-pollination among line and staff executives, including identification of problems and opportunities; (3) participation and exchange of ideas; (4) identification of practical applications of business fundamentals; (5) stimulation, inspiration, and intensified commitment; (6) follow-up and implementation throughout the corporation at both line and staff levels.

Length of the meeting. How long the meeting should run involves a number of considerations: who will be in attendance; how many are coming to such a meeting for the first time; what it will take to accomplish the stated objectives; whether there is ample time for recreation; the costs of an extra day; how long busy managers can afford to be gone from their jobs; the frequency of management meetings; and the attitudes of the top line and staff executives. There are other considerations, but consensus should decide and maximum benefits must be obtained by careful planning of each step and economizing on time.

At the meeting described, registration was scheduled to start on a Sunday afternoon. This allowed time for people to get acquainted socially, and there was specific provision for a variety of recreational activities. The evening included cocktails, dinner, introductions, announcements of new key promotions, and a good social period.

Two and one-half days were allotted to the meeting, with one entire afternoon off for recreation on the first full day (Monday) and a long recreation period (3 P.M. to 6 P.M.) on the second day. The meeting adjourned after a buffet lunch on the third day to allow ample time for participants to return to their respective homes. No evening meetings were held.

Planning for Participation and Involvement

For a company with homogeneous products, markets, customers, processes, and technology and with common problems and opportunities, it is easier to plan the priorities of topics to be covered in a management meeting, to summarize results against plans for the past year, and to develop strategies and tactics for the coming years. For a highly diversified conglomerate with relatively little intermingling of people, a different strategy is required to insure effective communication on a common ground.

Approximately half the meeting was taken up with points that had to be covered. These musts included keynote speeches of the chairman of the board and the president, who discussed corporate strategy and operating tactics in terms of objectives, organization and manpower strategy, financial and investment strategy, plans for growth and acquisitions, market strategy, and the day-to-day fundamentals which need to be executed with precision to insure realization of business results. Priorities were reaffirmed—for example, (1) avoid catastrophe, (2) improve profits, (3) plan for growth.

The reporting of the preceding year's results against planned goals was another must. This includes all operating divisions and groups as well as key staff executives. The manner of reporting can of course vary, and liberal use should be made of high-quality visual aids which can be seen clearly from the rear of the room. In the meeting in question, each president gave a brief synopsis of his financial results along with a brief commentary on the nature of his business, its problems and opportunities, and what he was doing or intending to do about them. These presentations were unusually well received.

One of the objectives of a management meeting is to get as many people involved as possible through participation in small group discussions. To insure a base of common interest, top line and staff executives were selected to give individual presentations—about eight minutes—each in the form of a panel discussion and were urged to bring out principles that are applicable to all businesses. The subject matter was developed accordingly and divided among the panel members. Dry runs were held at which most senior line and staff executives were present to critique and comment. A few questions were prepared to insure the start of a stimulating discussion in each group, which fortunately happened spontaneously anyway. These panel discussions were enthusiastically received, and many matters of policy were set on the table for subsequent follow-up.

Meetings were kept positive, yet the reports were not sugar-coated. A hard realistic look was taken at all phases of the business to insure the best practice of business fundamentals so as to be poised for future growth and improvement.

Meeting Evaluation

To seek improvements in subsequent meetings, a questionnaire was drawn up and sent to all who attended the meeting. The forms were to be returned anonymously so as to encourage frank comments. Questions were asked about the quality, length, and conduct of the meeting; reactions to the presentations of division managers; reactions to panel discussions; the benefits derived from the meeting; suggestions for future meetings; the adequacy of time, facilities, and accommodations;

and the planning, organization, and running of the meeting. An open-ended question was added soliciting comments.

Provision for Follow-up

To insure that the benefits of the meeting would be fully realized, the company president asked each participant to send him a listing of the four most useful business fundamentals which came out of the meeting. Exhibit 7-2 summarizes the 140 individual responses. In addition, each division manager and top corporate staff officer was asked to hold a follow-up meeting of his own with his people within three months of the conference. The human resources executive was made available to provide assistance and guidance in planning, setting up, and running these meetings. Of the 20 chief operating executives, 17 asked for and received assistance.

Typically, the field meetings were prepared for and conducted in this way. Letters were sent to all participants in advance of each scheduled meeting urging that they prepare to participate and be involved. Meetings were held off company premises and lasted two to four hours each. Meetings were set up in round-table fashion with pad and pencil, name tags, and 3″ × 5″ cards at each place. The division president opened the meeting by explaining purpose, objective, and format. Each participant had been sent an agenda in advance of the meeting. Taped excerpts of the chief executive officer's remarks at the earlier meeting were played and commented on, as these business fundamentals applied to the particular operation. Good and bad practices were stressed, but the comments ended on a positive, reassuring note.

Panel discussions were held by division marketing, manufacturing, controls, and human resources executives. There was a great deal of preparation beforehand, including a dry run. A secretary took minutes not only of presentations but of the active, lively discussions from the floor. The division president concluded and summarized the meeting and asked all participants to send him a note stating how they intended to improve the practice of business fundamentals in their operations during the coming year. Subsequent meetings were held at lower levels in each division.

Reactions were highly favorable and numerous expressions of appreciation and requests for similar future meetings were volunteered. The effect was to significantly improve the total organizational climate by providing a better understanding of each other's work and by opening up areas for further improvements in communication and working relationships. People became attuned to common goals.

Exhibit 7-2.
MOST USEFUL BUSINESS FUNDAMENTALS

MARKETING	MANUFACTURING	CONTROLS	HUMAN RESOURCES AND OTHER
Know your markets	Quantify and examine alternatives	Plan controls to help you manage your operations	Have superior people at all levels
Know your product	Weigh advantages and risks	Know where you have been, where you are, and where you are going	Set high performance standards for every position
Know your customers	Anticipate and plan for problems	Monitor and measure all critical facets of the business	Let people know how well they are doing
Know your competitors	Market needs determine products to be produced	Take timely action to keep on target; avoid catastrophe	Keep your promises
Watch your inventory	Know your manufacturing capabilities	Keep controls adequate, simple, timely, and properly implemented	Closely define your organization and each position
Know your inventory carrying costs	Know all your manufacturing costs	Tailor-make controls to fit your operations	Measure performance constantly
Do not sell ahead at a loss	Relate manufacturing costs to pricing considerations	Provide for information feedback	Plan for future growth
Admit when you are wrong	Maintain adequate flexibility in manufacturing equipment and facilities	Do not have excessive controls	Make your profit plan
Use marketing strengths of other divisions	Plan for and make intelligent adjustments to technological change	Use controls to achieve objectives, not as restraints	Have a detailed business plan
Know where your market or market segment is going for each product and brand	In evaluating capital expenditure proposals, define the market need and profit potential realistically	Use controls to concentrate marketing efforts on most profitable products, activities, and customers	Do not procrastinate
Know the location of each market you serve	• Examine alternatives	A good budget is the keystone of a good control system	Know your business
Know your weaknesses as well as your strengths	• Identify all costs on capital expenditures	Have controls that tell why as well as how and what	Find new ways to do your job better
Be conscious of your social, political, and economic environment	• Allow adequate time to achieve benefits	Have tight security on materials control	Establish priorities
Know your profitability and cost by product line	Base production plans on detailed marketing plans	Control scheduling of manpower and machines	Meet deadlines
Know your freight costs	Establish realistic inventory turnover goals	Control quantity of purchases and production	Motivate your people
Protect your market share	Adjust rapidly to changes in sales forecasts; act decisively		Balance long-range and short-term considerations
Get rid of the dogs in your product line			Plan how to get the job done and do it
Know the decision maker at each customer location			Get rid of unprofitable product lines, customers, facilities
Know your profitability by customer			Take prompt action
Use your strengths in making sales calls—reputation, delivery, quality, price, reliability			Spend money only to improve your business
			Don't panic
			Be aggressive and not defensive

MARKETING	MANUFACTURING	CONTROLS	HUMAN RESOURCES AND OTHER
Be honest in your business dealings	Act on prompt and complete knowledge of costs and efficiencies	Do not let bad product reach customer	Keep the show on the road
Know your competitors' costs, facilities, advantages, and disadvantages	Keep costs in line with revenues	Control hiring and use of people	Evaluate your risks to minimize exposure on the downside and maximize profits on the upside
Define your markets for each product precisely and know your position in each market and market segment	Expend the greatest effort on areas with greatest potential for cost improvement	Audit product quality to build quality into the product	Avoid clogging the paperwork pipelines
Is each market growing, shrinking, or moving sideways?	Have a continuing cost improvement program with assigned responsibilities	Control attendance	Be sure that status reports are meaningful and realistic
Know the probability of increasing the market share	Use all available systems for cost control	Use standard cost systems to highlight inefficiencies; take corrective action	Delegate authority
Improve your market forecasts	Give minimum acceptable quality at lowest cost	Control raw, in-process, and finished inventory levels; know what you have in stock	Communicate
Seek growth opportunities	Buy materials that cost no more than specifications require	Let each department know its costs of operations monthly against standards	Develop your people
Be honest in all dealings with customers, suppliers, and employees	When buying, negotiate!	Make controls inexpensive and uncomplicated	Respect people's points of view
Develop your sales people	Investigate your suppliers	Become involved in your operations	
Control your sales expenses and costs	Use quality control to eliminate causes of errors as opposed to rejecting products	Have the management team help set up and implement control systems	
	Set up formal preventive maintenance programs	Know your return on investment by product line	
	Identify areas of excess maintenance expense	Know all costs for each product	
	Have an adequate supply of vital utilities	Maintain minimum investment to satisfy customer needs	
	Make pollution control pay for itself	Watch your credits, collections, and credit risks	
	Use industrial engineering to improve productivity	Avoid big expense	

Organization Climate and Executive Orientation

When an executive is newly hired or is transferred to a different division, his introduction and orientation will influence his subsequent behavior and attitudes toward his own people and others and, hence, will exert a considerable impact on organization climate.

Like performance appraisal, socialization—or orientation—does take place, whether by accident or by design. Usually a series of events serves to undo old values and prepare the executive to learn new values. The process of unlearning can be an unpleasant experience and often requires strong motivation to endure it. If there are other newly hired executives, they will form a peer group to support organizational norms. Usually, this is not the case, and the executive learns from a variety of sources such as the official literature of his organization, the examples set by the behavior and demonstrated attitudes of other key executives, the instructions given to him by his boss, the examples of his peers who have been with the company for a long time, and the rewards and punishments which result from his own experimentation and efforts at problem solving.

This process often produces uncertainty and anxiety. Formal orientation sessions and company literature do not teach the organization's subtle values. While these may be well understood by senior management, they are often subtly communicated by peers: how the boss wants things done, what higher management thinks about issues and actions, and what things are considered heroic as well as what things are taboo.

On occasion, the values of the individual may not be consonant with the values of the organization. As an example, in most management consulting firms, productivity as measured by results achieved is the chief criterion for success. This is stressed accordingly in the orientation of new consultants because the product is the sale of professional counsel and advice. Yet sometimes bright, young, experienced consultants become so engrossed in providing client satisfaction that they tend to overlook the importance of developing harmonious internal relationships and integrating their efforts with those of other consultants and officers.

One creative young consultant, in the course of setting new records for individual productivity, broke a lot of china to find new shortcuts and killed a few sacred cows in the process.

Had the orientation procedure provided guidelines relative to establishing appropriate internal organizational relationships, this man could still have been with the company. When critical relationships, procedural matters, and policy guidelines are glossed over or not discussed, and day-to-day coaching with feedback of developmental needs is neglected, the organization climate produces anxiety and tension; relationships are strained, and eventually productivity is impaired and voluntary resignations increase.

Organizational socialization is supposed to build commitment and loyalty. This requires an investment of time and effort to earn the new employee's loyalty, encourage him to work hard, and facilitate his learning. The employee, in turn, will *want* to learn how to act in a way that will lead to acceptance and incorporation of company values.

New people are often frustrated because they are compelled to perform menial tasks that older members are unwilling to do themselves. The intent is to let them learn how the company really works before they take on an assignment with real responsibility. These transitional tasks are meant to help the new member incorporate new values, attitudes, and norms into his total experience. Finally the day comes when the new man is given real responsibility; confidences are shared with him and trust is shown in him and in his abilities. The new executive feels this strongly. He knows when he has been finally accepted. This could take a year or longer.

While most organizations place a premium on conformity, they do attach differing degrees of importance to their particular norms and value systems. Many of these are necessary for survival: doing a good job on time, having a profit orientation, following the proper channels of communication, seeking cost improvement as a way of business life. Others are desirable for compliance, such as manner of dress and appearance, living in the right neighborhood, belonging to the right club.

An organization has to focus on norms and values that are important for success and stop seeking and rewarding conformity to norms that have little relevance to results. This requires a positive and carefully planned sequence of experiences to orient new executives coming into the company. The really important organizational norms should not be learned by chance. If management comes to understand the process of socialization in its firm, it can use and control it to build a healthy environment.

An Ounce of Prevention . . .

Practitioners and students of management often compare the life cycle of an organization with that of a plant or of a human being. The length of time may vary, but both go through the distinct stages of birth, youth, maturity, old age, and death. While this is most vividly illustrated by a product life cycle, the same analogy can be drawn in looking at an entire organization. Yet in an organization, maturity can be maintained, and old age and death need not occur. This can be achieved by keeping an organizational climate healthy and thus preventing dry rot or calcification of the organization's vital organs.

One of the ways of doing this is by having a fresh stream of new ideas and new blood flowing into the organization at all levels. Not all positions should be filled from within. Such a policy could lead to complacency, rigidity, and effective closure of the door to new ways of doing things—new methods, processes, and techniques which can be introduced only by an outsider. The climate that is hospitable to the outsider is one that fosters change, welcomes it, requires constant, purposeful, progressive change as a way of life, and places a premium on creativity, not on conformity.

Most successful organizations that seem to go on and on, never aging, have the ability to criticize themselves and, in criticizing, seek new and constructive solutions to problems. They are able to react quickly to change and often precipitate change through new product introductions, new marketing approaches, and new techniques for human resources management.

The importance of a free flow and exchange of information upward, downward, and laterally cannot be overstressed. A vibrant organization is cognizant of what is happening to all its members, and it communicates matters of importance to all of them.

The healthy organization does not permit sacred cows to be created, sheltered, and protected at the expense of a favorable climate. It admits its muddles—and makes permanent corrections instead of expedient temporary cures.

The organization that stays young continually looks ahead; determines where it is going and how it will get there; and gets the people, programs, and projects to move it steadily forward.

The healthy organization continually assesses its own performance, has a simple early warning system that works, and effectively moves to change its plans, making intelligent adjustments as internal and external circumstances dictate. Time after time the organization demonstrates its capacity for self-renewal and thus avoids the specter of old age, obsolescence, and death.

8
Creative Management of the Human Resource

A great deal of space has been devoted thus far to effective management of the executive—a firm's managerial asset. This is not to slight the equally important concern of the human resources executive for the first-line supervisor, or the clerical employee, or the factory worker. The fact of the bimodal work force cannot be denied; it requires attention.

While the basic human relations principles do not vary significantly from one organizational level to the next, the approach and application of these principles do vary considerably. For example, there is no such thing as an effective universal plan of job evaluation.

The purpose now is to share a few experiences in providing human resource programs and satisfactions that have made companies better places in which to work. What follows will not be like a personnel director's handbook; instead, it describes a particularly difficult situation, tells what innovations in human resource management were tried, and reports the results of the experience. Since the chapter is geared to the lower organization levels, it seems appropriate to start with the first-line supervisor or foreman.

Often called the arms of management, the first-line supervisor finds that he is neither fish nor fowl. He is normally pulled from the ranks because of his superior productivity, and overnight he is expected to acquire the full range of skills and abilities of a supervisor. He must immediately plan, delegate, control, administer, measure, and follow up.

He finds himself torn by divided loyalties—to his fellow workers on the line and to his new manager. Often he has all kinds of responsibility, but relatively little authority. New and important relationships are introduced. The industrial engineer tells him how many people he will use, what equipment he should have, how the work is to flow through his shop, and the physical layout. A production planner or controller tells him how much of what is to be produced and when, where it will come from, how much is to be stored and how much shipped.

The personnel man says he cannot fire a poor employee, orders that he promote a man other than the one he wants, and often tells him who to hire and how the new employee is to be inducted into the workforce. He is also told how much the new man is to be paid and when he is eligible for an increase, as well as the size of the increase. The accountant tells him he spends too much money on gloves and supplies and his costs are out of line. The maintenance superintendent schedules his machines out of production for repair or overhaul, and the quality control inspector rejects his production because it does not meet the standards set by the engineering department. And, should the foreman find that despite all these "helpers" he is able to run smoothly, the salesman calls in a special order for an important customer; this disrupts the entire schedule and runs up costs.

For all this, the foreman takes home just slightly more money than his better workers. No wonder we find discontentment in this group. Foremen are management people and must be treated as such. We seem to do everything we can to make their jobs impossible. The least we should do is to prepare these men for what awaits them.

In a major appliance manufacturing firm, the need to carefully select and prepare candidates for first-line supervisory positions was recognized by the human resources executive, and something was done about it. The following is an actual case history.

The Problem

In the 1960s the mad scramble for exempt salaried personnel at all levels in most businesses forced many companies to appraise both short- and long-range manpower needs and devise plans and programs to meet these needs.

One manufacturer was acutely aware that well-trained candidates for foreman and other exempt manufacturing positions were not available from the open labor market. Priorities of needs had to be established; company policies of promotion from within needed further implementation. Because of a five-year projection of the needs for foremen in all manufacturing operations, this received top developmental priority. The projected need was for 29 foremen, 9 in assembly, 5 in fabrication, 3 in finishing, and 12 others. It was also shown that, of the 27 requests for foremen filled in the preceding two years, 10 had been outside hires and 17 had been promotions.

An exhaustive study of the foreman's job was made through a survey task force. Among the most significant findings from the survey, which was conducted to improve the effectiveness of the foreman from his point of view, were three expressed needs: (1) Upgrade from within, but give people training before putting them on the floor as foremen; (2) teach all foremen, especially newly appointed ones, all aspects of the foreman's job; (3) narrow the foreman's span of control to allow him more time with his people.

Faced with the need to add a second shift in at least two operating businesses, management recognized that informal training by means of the foreman-assistant approach was inadequate. A costly lesson had been learned. One of the three product businesses was selected to pilot a thorough, business-oriented foreman development program. Relations personnel obtained full approval and support from the department general manager to develop a sound constructive program.

The Approach

From conception to commencement of this program, six months elapsed. During this period, existing foreman training programs from other companies were examined in depth, and foremen and responsible managers from all functions were queried to ascertain their viewpoints on what should be included for a good foreman development program. Concurrent with program construction, plans were developed and implemented for candidate selection.

Each foreman in the pilot product department was asked to submit names of exceptional workers based on his personal assessment of their potential for promotion to exempt manufacturing positions. Factors such as productivity, quality of work, dependability, attitude, reliability, and judgment as defined on normal merit rating forms were used as criteria to aid in selection.

Of a total of 2,250 hourly employees in this product department, 143 names were submitted for consideration. From this nucleus of potential candidates, the first screening eliminated those who lacked a high school education or the equivalent as determined by the co-authors of this program: the manager–relations practices of the product department and the manager–personnel and manpower development. This first screening left 83 prospective candidates for the program.

At this point, each remaining candidate's foreman and general foreman spoke with him individually to notify him that he had been nominated for a manufacturing management development program. Each was given a general picture of the foreman's responsibilities, and an attempt was made to ascertain his interest and enthusiasm. The size of the group decreased to 41.

The next step in the selection process was to give each candidate a battery of tests to determine aptitudes, including mathematical reasoning ability, and general level of intelligence. The Purdue Shop Arithmetic test, the Wonderlic test, the Bennett Mechanical Comprehension test, and the SRA Nonverbal test were given, using the suggested norms for supervisory candidates. Fifteen candidates failed to make the grade. With the number of candidates now reduced to 26, a selection committee was established consisting of the superintendent, the manager–relations practices, the manager–personnel and manpower development, and a rotating shop operations supervisor at the general foreman level who did not participate in interviewing any of his own hourly people, but who interviewed candidates from other areas.

Candidates were scheduled to meet with the selection committee for approximately 20 minutes on company time. During this time, any member of the committee could ask any questions he felt were pertinent to ascertaining candidates' qualifications for foreman development. The questions, which began to take on a pattern, yielded such valuable information as candidates' concepts of orientation, training, and induction; human relations skills; technical knowledge; understanding of the foreman's job; tolerance for frustration and pressure; interest and enthusiasm; motivation; flexibility; and a host of related pertinent details, which each committee member recorded on an appropriate form. An example of this form is shown in Exhibit 8-1. The superintendent said he had been acquainted with several of the candidates for years, but he did not really come to know them until the interview.

By this time, candidates were developing the idea, as planned, that they were an elite group, carefully selected for a most important responsibility and opportunity. This attitude carried into the shop.

The committee ended up with 17 candidates. Each was sent a personal letter from the manager–personnel and manpower development telling him he had been selected to participate in the program, congratulating him, and asking him to indicate in writing whether he was willing to take part. All accepted. Top management suggested that the course also be offered to newly appointed foremen as an aid in their development, so new foremen were added to the group for cross-pollination of ideas and sharing of experiences.

Objective of the Program

Training was focused on the philosophy of developing broad-gauge supervisors with a sound business orientation who could assume re-

Exhibit 8-1.
SELECTION COMMITTEE RATING FOR FOREMAN DEVELOPMENT PROGRAM

Name ________________________ Date ____________

1. *Applicant's characteristics:*

A.	Attitude:	☐ Excellent ☐ Good ☐ Fair ☐ Poor	B.	Desire:	☐ Excellent ☐ Good ☐ Fair ☐ Poor	C.	Self-confidence (poise): ☐ Outstanding ☐ Above Average ☐ Average ☐ Poor
D.	Decision-making ability:	☐ Excellent ☐ Good ☐ Satisfactory ☐ Poor	E.	Personal appearance:	☐ Outstanding ☐ Above Average ☐ Average ☐ Poor	F.	Overall rating: ☐ Superior ☐ Above Average ☐ Average ☐ Poor

2. *Personnel information*
   - Age:
   - Education grade:
   - Current job:
   - Current job rate:
   - C/S date:
   - Marital status:
   - Military service:

3. *Raw test scores* / *Cutoff scores*

Raw test scores		*Cutoff scores*
Bennett		
Mechanical Comprehension	________	________
Purdue Shop Arithmetic	________	________
Wonderlic	________	________
SRA Nonverbal	________	________

4. *Recommendations:*

   Accept
   Yes ☐ No ☐

5. *Additional comments:* ________________________

____
Selection Committee Member

sponsibilities in any one of a variety of manufacturing positions with additional training. Typical positions which incumbents were to fill included foreman, dispatcher, buyer, production control analyst, product scheduler, and methods and time standards technician.

To provide broad-gauge training and knowledge of the total business required careful study of each of its component parts. Specific objectives which determined essential elements of the curriculum included the following: (1) Provide a breadth of knowledge of the specific responsibilities of the foreman's position; (2) enable each participant to develop an understanding of the organization of the business and how each function relates to each other as well as to the shop; (3) provide opportunities to share experiences with each other through class discussion, role playing, and case studies with the purpose of developing a sound approach to the solution of problems in the factory; point out how to utilize all the services available to the foremen inside and outside of manufacturing to do a more effective job.

Course Content

Once objectives had been agreed to and established, attention could be turned to the dual task of selecting instructors and defining specific sessions. Need determined course length and content.

It was decided to utilize general management as well as functional management and individual contributors. To illustrate the high level of support which was obtained, department general management initiated the program and pledged full support in person. As one department general manager put it, "If this weren't important, I wouldn't be here."

Each participant was given a copy of the course outline in a suitably inscribed three-way binder with ample space for notes and handouts. Classes met once a week from 4 P.M. to 6 P.M. The program guide follows.

Session	TOPIC	SPEAKER
1	Company history, organization, and operating philosophy and the business section's role in the appliance industry	General Manager–Business Section
2	Marketing our products; competition; selling techniques	Manager–Marketing
3	Financial side of business: budgets, measurements, and cost control	Manager–Finance
4	Engineering department: design and evaluation	Manager–Engineering

Session	TOPIC	SPEAKER
5	Employee motivation	Outside consultant
6	Manufacturing operations: discussion of production including organization, job responsibilities, and co-operative role of other functions	Manager–Manufacturing
7	What is the shop?	Consultant–Internal Manufacturing Services
8	Manufacturing engineering: introduction to the function and its contribution to manufacturing	Manager–Manufacturing Engineering
9	Materials control: purchasing, expediting, inventory control, and utilization of purchased and manufactured parts	Manager–Materials
10	Production control: product scheduling, dispatching, and control of production	Supervisor–Production Control
11	Fundamentals of methods and time standards and wage payment	Supervisor–Process and Time Standards Engineer
12	Employment and unemployment in the area	U.S. Department of Labor Representative
13	Workshops: meeting in small groups for two one-hour periods to review what has been discussed to date; leaders elected from each group	
14	Principles of quality control: procedures involving foremen; their responsibility for quality planning and control	Supervisor–Quality Control
15	Developing and accomplishing work goals; how work planning helps a foreman do a better job Advance assignment: Describe what you look for in a new employee and how you would induct him into the workforce.	Manager–Personnel
16	The foreman's job as viewed by management and program participants Advance assignment: Develop a work plan for a foreman in your work area.	Superintendent
17	Manpower selection and training: description of the employment process and methods of training new employees Advance assignment: Prepare questions on wage administration policy which you would like to have answered.	Manager–Personnel and Manpower Development
18	Compensation practices: role of foreman in wage practices and payroll problems	Wage Administration Consultant
19	Discipline and control: the foreman's role in maintaining discipline Advance assignment: Prepare a case study of an actual discipline problem.	Union Relations Specialist
20	Union relations: a review of contracts, grievance procedure, and collective bargaining Advance assignment: Keep a log of one full day's activities, noting every communication, written and oral.	Manager–Union Relations

Session	TOPIC	SPEAKER
21	Communication: elements and techniques of effective communication	Manager–Communication and Community Relations
22	Summary of the role of the foreman; complete review of the foreman's manual pointing up subjects previously discussed	Union Relations Specialist
23	Case study: a typical situation involving a foreman and how he solves his daily problems	Staff and participants
24	Graduation ceremonies and banquet	

Instructor Selection and Training

Potential instructors were identified on the basis of demonstrated achievements in their areas of proficiency as well as formal education. Curriculum content dictated the choice of managers. Each potential instructor was sent a letter from the general manager indicating that he had been selected and asking that he accept this additional responsibility.

> Our business operation is commencing a foreman development program. The purpose of this program is to develop capable people with high potential for future open exempt manufacturing positions.
>
> Because of your experience and knowledge, you have been designated as a potential discussion leader for one of the sessions: Other discussion leaders will include outside consultants from manufacturing services and from the U.S. Department of Labor. They have accepted. It would be a real service to us if you would accept this assignment. You can contribute a great deal to the program.
>
> I have asked our manager of manpower development, who will coordinate this program, to contact you to determine your interest in participation, define and discuss the role you would play, and review the curriculum with you.
>
> Please give him your full cooperation in this most important development program.

The response was overwhelmingly enthusiastic. The following guide, which was sent to all the session leaders, covers some of the considerations discussed with them.

> Please review the attached curriculum very carefully to insure that your discussion relates to the whole program. Gear your presentation to the level of preforemen and new foremen. The program outline,

as you will note, could well apply to general foremen and superintendents. Do not lose your audience.

Prepare thoroughly and completely. An inadequate presentation, off the cuff, can do more harm than good. The participants will sense the lack of preparation and will respond accordingly. Use visual aids and handouts.

Where there is a case study or role-playing situation involved, you will be given assistance in preparing this part of your session and in appropriate teaching techniques to insure participation and involvement and to help in evaluation of participants' efforts.

If you are instructing a session which includes an advance assignment at the end, you will be provided with additional information relative to the assignment. This is important because it sets the stage for the material to be covered by the next discussion leader. Should you be on the receiving end of such an assignment, the relationship to your session is obvious.

Sessions must begin and end on time; be prompt. Allow a ten-minute coffee break at 5:10 P.M.—coffee will be provided. Learning and retention are enhanced when there is a short break between periods.

One last consideration: You will be asked to submit two questions to summarize learning of material included in your session. Additionally, you may be asked to evaluate the students relative to their participation and contribution to class discussions and special written assignments. It is therefore important that your session content be so constructed as to elicit a variety of participant responses. The curriculum is arranged to make this easier for you.

Each session was attended by the program coordinators and a corporate trainee. Weekly feedback was actively solicited, both favorable and unfavorable; needed changes were made immediately so as to improve subsequent instructors' effectiveness of presentation and discussion. The formal weekly audits and one class appraisal midway through the course covered such items as presentation, use of audiovisual aids, instructors' delivery, class participation, value of handouts, contribution of material, and suggestions for improvement.

Benefits and Measurements

After six months of preparation, the program was in full stride. It was of course recognized that the ultimate test would be the success or failure of the graduates in exempt assignments. Notwithstanding this, new levels of self-confidence soon became evident. The class recognized a deficiency in shop math, so 13 students petitioned the program coordinator to offer a course in shop math on their own time. A course *was* arranged; it was held on company premises on the employees' own time (comparable to the foreman development program); all 13 participants completed this additional program, taught by a certified teacher from the local board of education.

There are other early tangible results of this experiment. Several participants were promoted to open foreman positions; their performance was superior to that of foremen previously selected. There is now less concern at the top level of management about filling the need for qualified foremen. Present foremen and manufacturing management have demonstrated great interest in the program. The program coordinator has been asked to develop a similar program for the other two product businesses.

There was virtually no absenteeism or tardiness in the factory on the part of the participants, and absenteeism has been significantly reduced in their sections. A follow-up program was planned and implemented for graduates. It was designed to further develop and improve individual leadership styles. In short, the problem of foreman recruitment and development at the appliance manufacturer has been solved.

Improvement of the Foreman's Position

When management is confronted with serious problems such as a sudden increase in manufacturing costs, it often overlooks the obvious approach to a solution: going directly to the supervisors at the first line, where the dollars are spent, to find out what has gone wrong and why.

This next experience represents the efforts of a few human resources executives who recognized that high manufacturing costs could probably be associated directly with increased labor costs. Because employees are directly supervised by the foreman, he is a focal point in determining the causes for the increased costs and what can be done to reduce these costs to a more acceptable level.

In this example, there was a variety of contradictory opinions relative to the nature of the problems in the foremen's areas and the approaches to be taken to resolve these problems and thus reduce excessive costs. The human resources executive was able to persuade top management that these problems could be resolved only if a true appraisal was made of the present status of the foreman position, with all its attendant problems. Top management commissioned the human resources executive to make this study, and he selected his own team. The time allotted was short, and good results had to be obtained.

The objectives of the study team were twofold: first, identify the forces, if any, which hamper the effectiveness of the foreman and diminish his motivation; second, come up with recommendations for removing these negative forces and thus bringing excess costs down to a reasonable, acceptable limit. Major emphasis was placed on production foremen.

Because of the limitations of time, the personal interview technique was adopted by the study team. In all, 33 individuals were interviewed: 19 foremen and 14 manufacturing superintendents and managers. A series of questions was devised to start discussions; once started, additional questions on the same subject were asked to ascertain the full scope of the problem and to elicit suggested solutions. Starter questions included these:

- Has the foreman's position changed in the past two years? If it has, in what important ways?
- Has the foreman's responsibility increased, decreased, or remained the same in the past two years? If it has changed, in what important ways?
- Does the present management organization exert an influence on the foreman's position? If so, explain how.
- Is the present organization of the factory sound and effective? If not, in what specific ways can it be improved?
- What are the major problems facing the foreman today? How would you solve these problems?
- Where should management get men to fill foremen's positions?
- Are new foremen adequately trained? If not, how can training be improved?
- Do foremen receive proper assistance and guidance from the managers to whom they report? If not, in what ways can management be improved?
- Is present communication with the foreman sufficient and effective? If not, how could it be improved?
- What can management do to improve the foreman's position?
- What is the foreman's present attitude toward his job and the company?
- How does the foreman feel about his pay, his organizational level, and his status?

The technique was very well received and cooperation was exceptional. Individuals were told that their responses would be kept confidential, and there appeared to be little holding back.

The information obtained from these interviews was pooled with an earlier foremen's attitude survey, comparative salary surveys, and exit interviews of minority group employees who had voluntarily left the company. The information generated from these interviews and other sources seemed to divide itself into five major areas: the foreman's position, recruitment and training, communication, pay and recognition, and attitudes. The following summaries represent the consensus of all interviewed.

The *foreman's position.* Of those queried, 88 percent answered that while the results expected were demanding, they were in fact reasonable. The men expressed concern about a number of factors that limited their effectiveness. Specifically, several foremen noted that they frequently found themselves occupied with securing materials, tools, and services which had not been supplied according to schedule. This pulled them away from their work areas and from their responsibilities of training, directing, communicating, and tending to their people's needs. More clerical help was needed to administer the timekeeping and ratekeeping aspects of the hourly incentive system. Many foremen complained about poor services and shortages of materials and parts. Many also felt that they were overextended to the point where they were unable to perform effectively. Increased production schedules not only strained the facilities but caused line backups and parts shortages. When more people were assigned, more attention was required for each person. The span of control averaged 45 people, with a high of 90 and a low of 11. The number should not have exceeded 35 for optimum efficiency and control.

There just was not enough time in the day to do everything that needed to be done. The number of models being built and the frequency of schedule changes had increased significantly. These new models were more demanding and required extra attention. The so-called new breed of employee also required more attention. By the "new breed" was meant the minority group employees whose attitudes toward their work and their foremen and whose sense of responsibility seemed to be the cause of poorer quality and lower quantity of output than had been the norm. Extra time was needed to train and motivate them. Since their arrival, absenteeism had increased from 2.4 percent to 4 percent, garnishments—or wage assignments—had increased from 20 to 50 a week, and the number of incidences that required disciplinary action had doubled. For every employee recruited and kept working, three people had to be put on the payroll. Turnover had reached disastrous proportions.

Absenteeism necessitated frequent transfer of new employees, which was disturbing to them and costly to the company. This contributed to high turnover. "The new employees just don't seem to care" was the general complaint. While the basic responsibilities of the foremen remained about the same, the problems had become numerous and complex, resulting in poor quality, low productivity, and missed schedules.

Recruitment and training. As business expanded, as foremen grew older, and as new employees required additional supervision, there was concern as to where the new foremen would come from because it was virtually impossible to recruit from outside. The foremen themselves felt that there were good candidates in the ranks, even among newly hired employees. Everywhere, there was concern about additions and replacements. Among those needed were not only foremen but production control people, time standards personnel, and dispatchers.

Previous efforts at training new foremen were haphazard and usually consisted primarily of "assistant to" assignments for a brief period before being appointed foremen. The general comment was: "We need more classroom work as well as on-the-job training to handle the complexities of the foreman's job, including the incentive system and the union contract." The solution was foreman development. What the foremen themselves described as problems during these sessions formed the basis for the course.

Communication. It was agreed that the foreman who is aware of the general business situation and what is happening in his department is without doubt better prepared to do his job, even though he could operate effectively without this knowledge. However, if the foreman is not aware of changes in schedule, holdups in delivery of parts or supplies, or shortages of needed tools, the immediate consequences are apparent and costly. If he knows what is affecting his day-to-day operations, he can communicate this to his people and prevent problems.

While the foremen appreciated the conferences and management newsletters, they felt a real need to get more precise information from their immediate managers on the day-to-day running of the business. Specifically, they complained about not being informed of schedule changes in sufficient time to make adjustments in an orderly, economical manner. They pointed out the need for better communication between shop areas to permit them to make schedule changes. Out of 50 responses in a prior attitude survey, 25 noted a need for improvement in operational communication. The typical comment was that "day-to-day problems have to be communicated sooner and understood better." The physical communications facilities were poor, and an intercom system was needed.

Pay and recognition. The contribution made by foremen to overall profitability has to be clearly reflected in the salaries paid to them.

But pay alone, even when it is more than fair and equitable, is not sufficient for most of us, and on this score foremen are no different. They also seek the symbols of status, the words of praise, and the association with those above them in the organization that satisfy their desire for recognition.

The foremen's immediate managers were concerned with the relationship of a foreman's pay to that of his people, particularly where overtime is a big factor in determining gross pay. The foreman is keenly aware of any deficiencies since he passes out his people's checks. Most of the foremen interviewed did not say they considered their salaries too low. But a number of them thought it would be better if there were a greater span to compensate for additional responsibility and complexity of duties.

When many hours of overtime were worked by both foremen and workers, the salary differential was adjudged to be too low. When overtime was not scheduled, it was not compensated for. This was resented as arbitrary and unfair.

The main point the foremen brought out with regard to recognition was the lack of adequate private office space. Most foremen were satisfied with the authority and dignity of their jobs and the support of management.

Attitudes. No matter how good conditions may actually be, if the foreman views them pessimistically and considers his work an exercise in frustration, all his work and all his relationships will be negatively affected. Conversely, if his viewpoint is optimistic, his expressed attitude will reflect a genuine interest in his work and in the company.

Despite the adverse conditions just described, the foremen generally viewed their jobs as good jobs and regarded the company as a good place to work. While this view was not necessarily expressed positively in all instances, it was implied by the general absence of strong criticism. In a previous survey, more than 80 percent of 50 foremen stated they were satisfied with their own managers as well as with the type of work they were doing. In addition, 70 percent felt that they were treated as an important part of the management team. In turn, more than 80 percent of the managers felt that the foremen had a good attitude toward their jobs.

The study team of three people never lost sight of the prime original objective: to maximize the effectiveness of the foremen in order to minimize the excessive manufacturing costs. It was also recognized that some costs would be incurred to put the recommendations into effect. Generally, the magnitude of the solution was in direct proportion to the magnitude of the problem. Recommendations were divided into those for immediate implementation—a measure of the urgency of the problem—and others of longer-term duration.

Recommendations for Immediate Implementation

Assign to each foreman a package of work which he is able to perform. In order for a foreman to do his job properly, the demands on his time must be brought within reasonable bounds. Each foreman's position was reviewed by the manufacturing manager and the human resources executive to make this determination. The span of control for each foreman was reviewed to ascertain whether he had too many people and could not get to know each one or effectively manage and administer the group. The general guidelines decided on were 40 for assembly and finishing, 30 for fabrication and machining. If the numbers appeared satisfactory, the physical location of the people was reviewed to see whether these could be supervised effectively. In some cases, a cost improvement was effected by having an hourly rated leader or senior operator provide work direction for an area.

Additionally, if the number of hourly rated controlmen or other senior hourly rated employees was not sufficient to free foremen from minor decisions such as quality checks, need for more parts, or ways to perform an operation, these people were added by upgrade from within the ranks. They were then clearly instructed in what they were authorized to do and not to do, and the foreman concurred in this delegation of authority.

Until the foreman development program could produce candidates, foreman trainees were assigned in areas of excessive work to supervise groups that required more attention than the foreman was able to give them. These trainees were more than just assistants-to who sat at the foreman's elbow; they were assigned direct areas of responsibility with full authority and accountability.

Specific goals were identified to improve services to the foremen. Where there was a deficiency in vital services—slow parts delivery, inadequate tool servicing, defective materials—the responsible manager established the specific steps to improve these services so as to relieve the foremen of the expediting duties which they had had to assume to accomplish their basic production task. The whole area of materials control was carefully audited, and the best talent was assigned to make it more effective.

Relieve the foreman of responsibilities that could be performed more efficiently and more economically by others. One of the common complaints of foremen had to do with the necessity to process a large volume of clerical work such as timekeeping which could be done by clerical people if they were available. Foremen should sign voucher sheets and exception payments, but not routine reports. Briefly, it was determined how much clerical help was really required by each foreman, and provision was made to obtain that help.

Adjust current manufacturing practices and procedures to accommodate the new personnel being recruited. It was recognized that more managerial care and attention was required in recruiting and in manufacturing to make more effective use of newly hired employees. New practices were designed to get a more selective group of new employees into the factory and then give them more care and attention than previously.

Three specific measures were established. The first was development of an employment program to be administered by the human resources executive; its purpose was to acquaint new employees with factory work and working conditions, thus influencing their basic attitudes and attuning them to the demands of factory employment. This eventually became a one-day induction or employment entry program.

The second step was to hire a full-time counselor, reporting to the human resources executive, to work on the problem of absenteeism and its causes and cure. He spent his time following up daily and counseling with absentees to get them to realize the necessity for prompt, daily attendance. While this is normally the first-line supervisor's responsibility, the high incidence of absenteeism coupled with the stringent demands on the foreman's time and the difficulties in communicating with disadvantaged employees necessitated the employment of a counselor for optimum handling. Absenteeism was cut from more than 4 percent to 3 percent and thus reduced a number of associated problems.

The third step was to train key hourly rated people in job instruction techniques and the specifics of assembling new models so they would be better prepared to train and assist personnel on the line as new models were introduced. Major improvement in quality and production resulted, with attendant reduction in scrap and rework.

Identify and train the necessary potential foremen. While the need for more supervisors was never questioned, the means of satisfying this need had to be found. As described in the previous section, it was agreed by line and staff that manufacturing supervisors and foremen identify all their hourly people who appeared to have the knowledge, experience, and personality necessary to qualify them for a foreman's job or for some other exempt salaried manufacturing position. As the experiment was described, candidate interest also became a major factor in selection. The curriculum was the result of a joint effort of manufacturing executives and the human resources executive.

Improve the timeliness and accuracy of production change information communicated between manufacturing components. This problem seemed to be confined primarily to the procedures, mechanics, and timing involved in communicating information between manufacturing components. The materials management director was assigned to review the current flow of documents and other communications to determine whether to improve the current system or to change the system itself. Some changes were also made in the physical facilities for speeding up transmission of information among components. Most problems were solved within the existing system.

Pay foremen an overtime premium for scheduled overtime worked. A new procedure was instituted which provided for payment of all scheduled overtime hours worked by foremen. The overtime payment was to be on a straight time basis, computed on each man's equivalent hourly rate of pay. This was especially well received by foremen and made possible a real differential between the foreman's check and those of his highest paid hourly people. In addition, a survey of comparable local manufacturing firms was made, in person, by the compensation specialist, to exchange data on foremen's salaries in order to correct any out-of-line situations. It was found that the company compared very favorably, being on the high side in most instances.

Provide foremen with private office space in which to conduct their interviews and complete their paperwork assignments. Arrangements were made to construct offices at several key areas in the plant where foremen could write up pay vouchers, prepare written answers to suggestions and grievances, and conduct employee interviews in private. This served to enhance the status of the foremen in the eyes of their employees and to relieve their feelings of status incongruence.

In addition, on the matter of status, the human resources executive was given responsibility for planning and sponsoring a number of social and educational management outings each year to which foremen were specifically invited; here they could mingle with senior management in an informal, yet constructive, management association.

Communicate results of the survey to the foremen. Often a foreman participates in a survey or a study project, but is not told the results. The results of this study along with the recommendations to be implemented were communicated to all foremen and their managers in informative meetings conducted jointly by the manager of manufacturing and the human resources executive. This served to make the foremen more aware of top management's concern for their needs and appreciation for their contributions. It also conveyed management's intention to make the foreman's position better, less frustrating, and more appreciated.

The Results, in Sum

Foremen were considered to be professionals even while recognizing that they had limited opportunity for advancement into the upper echelons of management. The development of performance standards for each foreman position, the introduction of rotational assignments, and the transfer of superior foremen to positions of responsibility in manufacturing, industrial engineering, or materials management provided additional recognition and opportunity on the basis of demonstrated accomplishment, ability, and potential. Outstanding foremen were given additional recognition in the form of managerial awards in cash and stock, over and above merited salary adjustments. Achievements were thoroughly communicated, and additional avenues of advancement were opened up without distortion of the basic organization structure. Thus the problems of excessive costs were solved through innovative approaches to improving the job.

Testing Without Tests in Hiring the Disadvantaged

Higher turnover rates. Lower productivity. Poorer quality. Negative attitudes existed among hourly rated employees who are starting factory work for the first time. That these problems have been on the rise with the influx of minority group employees is no secret. One manufacturer, with turnover costs of $400 per employee and a record of hiring three new employees to net one, set out to improve its selection procedures in an effort to reduce its astronomical turnover costs.

A number of management executives had been exposed to testing procedures as preselection and screening devices. They conveyed the hope to the human resources executive that turnover could be reduced by 25 percent with other indirect advantages if a good testing program were initiated. Characteristically, management has expected too much from tests and often uses them as a substitute for making judgments based on more relevant data such as a man's "track record."

It is a well-known fact that in the past testing has established its validity and reliability in terms of identifying characteristics of successful employees in relation to specific job requirements and thus has provided criteria for selection and prediction of successful on-the-job performance. The question was: "Could testing procedures be used to predict performance among disadvantaged youths and adults, in this particular environment, for minority groups who for the most part were getting their first exposure to factory life?"

To determine scientifically whether testing would solve the turnover problem by screening out undesirable employment risks, the human resources executive called in a well-known psychological consultant to help set up a plan. Keeping in mind the work that needed to be done and the areas of highest turnover, the two selected tests that were designed to measure skills required in such areas as assembly, fabrication, and conveyor line work.

Such tests, validated for comparable kinds of work, involved measuring, vocabulary or general intelligence, precision, coordination, and assembly comprehension. A nonverbal test was also included. The tests had to be administered to groups. They take approximately 30 to 45 minutes to complete and are easily scored and interpreted.

A group of some 300 randomly selected hourly employees were initially tested, and foremen evaluated the performance of each individual as to dependability, attitude, judgment, and quality and quantity of work. While these evaluations were somewhat subjective, they were checked against production records. The test scores and actual performance evaluations were computed and correlated by an outside research firm.

In addition to the employee group of 300 people, some 600 job applicants were given the same battery of tests. All were hired because test validity and reliability could be established only by initially *not* using the tests as a screening device; they had to be used later in company performance records.

The newly hired employees' performance was evaluated after they had been on the job for two to three months. Many had already quit or been discharged prior to the evaluation, but the sample size was sufficiently large to serve as a valid measure.

After the first battery of tests was completed and checked, a comparison of test scores and on-the-job performance revealed that *no* tests predicted very well for people between 28 and 41 years of age.

For this test group, which consisted primarily of minority group employees, the nonverbal test made the best contribution, but had little predictive value. While it was hoped that one or a combination of tests might yield a lower and/or an upper limit of scores beyond which the individual would not be hired, this did not occur. Precision and coordination tests were excluded because of their extremely low correlation to performance.

It was significant that none of the tests correlated very well with the three variables which were deemed most important: overall performance rating, tenure, and potential for rehiring. The coefficients of correlation with both groups were so low—in some cases negative—that the tests would not be valid or reliable.

The conclusion arrived at by the human resources executive and his team was that by using recommended norms, the best that could be hoped for would be to reject approximately 10 percent of the potential quits or discharges. This did not warrant the time or the effort, and it was obvious that another solution had to be found.

This experiment with testing by no means served to invalidate the use of tests in predicting performance and tenure; rather, it could be hypothesized that the possibilities of cultural bias (even in nonverbal tests), the anxieties experienced by employees and applicants in mass hiring programs, the lack of appropriate employment and induction procedures, the pressures on first-line supervisors, and a host of other factors could well have contributed to the inability to develop a good predictive tool.

The Application Blank as a Predictive Tool

In conjunction with two in-house behavioral research psychologists, the human resources executive undertook a study of the company's application blank to determine whether any items would prove to identify a potential "stay" or a potential "quit."

Experiences with weighted application blanks in the past have proved them to be successful devices in identifying the particular characteristics of those employees who were most likely to stay as opposed to those who were most likely to quit. Would a particular combination of characteristics prove to be valid and reliable in working with this particular group of applicants in this particular labor market at this time? An attempt was made to answer these questions.

For this study, the application blanks of more than 1,000 employees hired in a single calendar year were analyzed with the objective of determining the predictability of turnover by pinpointing common characteristics of stays and quits. This identification was to be made by statistically interpreting variables common to employees in either group. The majority of hires during the calendar year in question were minority group employees.

Length of employment was an important factor in this study. For example, for approximately half the group considered in the first part of the study it was determined that 51.6 percent or 373 employees terminated their services within 31 days and 124 or 17.7 percent terminated after three or more months of service. Both groups were studied—the short-term and long-term quits—to find the common characteristics or significant variables for the two groups.

The *stay group* was defined as those with six months or more of continuous service. There were 615 in this group. Six months was selected as the cutoff period because the likelihood of turnover diminished if an employee made it for six months. These characteristics or factors on the application blank were analyzed: telephone, community area, months of residence in community, birthplace, housing, marital status, dependents, sex, age, citizenship, medical history, record of arrests, education, special training, desired position, position assigned as requested, earnings specified, shift preference, received shift preference, employee referral, military service, total jobs held, excluding military service, total months on last job and on longest job, months unemployed between last job and date of employment, previous factory work experience, months on unemployment compensation, continuity of factory occupation, salary progression, spelling, ability to follow instructions, test scores, termination of previous employment, total months on job as indicated on employment application.

Contrary to what had been expected, no variable could be identified as a characteristic of a stay as compared with a quit for possible use in a redesigned weighted screening instrument. The sample had failed to produce positive predictions. It appeared that the applicants had supplied information which tended to be typical of random living.

One bright spot emerged: Eliminating the application blank as a screening device saved a great deal of time for interviewers who had to process approximately 100 people a week.

To attempt to explain the failure of this previously tried and proven technique, the same rationale might be applied as the hypothesis as to why testing did not, in this instance, produce the desired results. It is quite possible that there were too many other negative variables at work, both in the employment process and in the work situation, that could easily have served to invalidate an otherwise intelligent technique to assist in the preemployment screening process. It became obvious that other techniques had to be tried as a means of reducing separations.

Examining the Procedures for Hiring Hourly Employees

When the study of application blanks failed to yield significant data, the study team turned its attention to hourly employees and the processes of hiring them. This part of the total approach to reducing turnover had as its objectives a definition of the employment system, an examination of the effectiveness of selection and placement practices, and recommendations for improvement. Information was obtained through personal observation, interviews, and examination of existing personnel records.

The first question to be examined was, what groups were causing the turnover? It was found that blacks contributed to terminations at about the same rate that they contributed to hires. Spanish-speaking people contributed to terminations at a rate 5 percent lower than they contributed to hires. Caucasians had the worst record, contributing to terminations at a rate 50 percent higher than they contributed to hires. Thus Caucasians were the highest turnover risk, while Spanish-speaking people were the lowest turnover risk.

Second, patterns of length of service were examined. Contrary to popular belief, half of all new hires who terminated had one month of service or less. In fact, one-fifth of all terminations occurred within one week of hiring, and the overall turnover rate was accelerating. Because the first day, week, and month of service were shown to be extremely critical periods, it seemed reasonable to assume that innovations to reduce turnover should be directed toward this time. Four to six months of service witnessed a considerable leveling off of turnover.

Turnover was not uniform among departments. Something, in fact, was happening in the environment to cause major differences. Perhaps it was the nature of the work itself, the physical environment, the foreman's leadership style, pay rates, shift, degree of training, degree of orientation, communication practices, composition of the work group, demands placed on foremen by higher management, advancement opportunities, or type of job.

The best and the worst units were examined in detail to identify good practices that should be incorporated and bad practices that should be eliminated in the orientation and induction processes throughout the shop. Dramatic differences between units proved to be a valuable clue in reducing turnover through restructuring and reevaluating jobs.

Another step was to check out terminations and hires to find out whether the month of the year made any difference. No significant difference was found between months. This analysis did help to increase the sensitivity of the data as it was discovered that one-fifth of all hires left the company within the first week and almost one-third left before reaching two months of service.

Projections based on changes in the composition of the workforce indicated that blacks would soon become the majority group of hourly employees. This could generate a secondary wave of turnover if management did not make ample preparations.

Management increased its efforts in many ways to understand blacks better and allocated necessary additional resources for supervision and training. Blacks who had the qualifications were enrolled in the foreman development program, as an example.

Increased business became a major issue because it was believed that many of the problems resulted from major workforce buildup within relatively short periods of time. During these periods, the emphasis necessarily had to shift from quality to quantity. Getting "warm bodies" in to work the lines became the *only* criterion for success in the personnel office. Absenteeism, turnover, poor quality, low productivity, and unfavorable attitudes were built into this approach.

A great deal of attention was focused on the first month of employment. It was first suggested that the high number of voluntary and forced resignations resulted from management's early identification of severely underqualified employees. The data revealed that many employees discovered early in the game that they had come into a hostile environment, and they did not like the way they were treated.

The analysis of the hiring process gave clear evidence of a lack of realistic objectives for both short- and long-range needs of management and employees in terms of ethnic, skill, age, and sex mix. In other words, before the personnel function could get the necessary resources, it had to know what was wanted and what was needed in order to end up with qualified personnel. It was later decided, for example, to substitute "learnability" for experience as a criterion for employment. As a result, new sources for labor were developed and successfully used to reduce turnover. For example, the language barrier was surmounted in the case of Spanish-speaking people.

While there was evidence of some manpower planning, the involvement of the personnel function had been too little and too late. Forecasts were inaccurate, further compounding the problem. (This was dramatically reversed, with the human resources executive playing a pivotal role in manpower planning and development.) Coupled with all this, the personnel office had unrealistically assessed its capacity to handle crash buildups without sacrificing existing hiring standards. Top management became directly involved from that point on.

Specific support activity was subsequently secured by means of communications to employees, local public high schools, trade schools, and vocational schools as well as public, fraternal, social, welfare, and service organizations. The help of all was systematically enlisted, and the enthusiastic response helped to solve the problem. A study of the company image in the community was undertaken by a private consultant, and the findings were used partially to redirect recruiting efforts. An integrated plan and recruiting effort was developed which identified what to do, by whom, and when, as well as what resources were necessary. Co-op programs were developed with local high schools for factory positions. This worked very well.

Entirely new sources were tapped and evaluated to assist recruiting efforts. Such sources included the company dealer organization, the welfare department, local public unemployment compensation offices, former employees, young adult organizations, new immigrants, early retirees, sunlighters, and moonlighters. This aggressive integrated campaign which witnessed the establishment of satellite interviewing stations tapped new sources of employees and provided a steady stream of new applicants. Employee referrals were used appropriately, as another example. And classified advertising was placed in a variety of ethnic publications as well as in daily newspapers.

The Employment System Itself

The facilities were completely inadequate to handle the high volume of applicants and to attract, select, and "screen in" good applicants. As the labor supply changed, the company had stayed with its existing policies, systems, and resources even though these were insufficient to do the job. The apparent willingness to accept underqualified employees and then not do anything to improve their qualifications created many problems.

Major changes were initiated and implemented, including the data and timing on the personnel requests which spelled out job requirements. All essential information had to be provided by the supervisor requesting help, or the request was sent back. Realistic lead time was allowed, and demands were brought into reasonable control.

The facility and the environment were changed, and in some cases the people were trained to change an indifferent and occasional hostile environment into a pleasant, welcoming environment. All systems and paperwork were simplified, the number of applicant visits was reduced, privacy was introduced, and delays were minimized. The situation was structured to meet the needs of applicants instead of ignoring them. Several forms were consolidated into one to save time and improve efficiency in paperwork processing. The whole system was improved.

The Orientation Survey

Once the employment system was straightened out and corrected, attention was next focused on the processes by which a new employee was inducted into a shop. A sample of 50 foremen and 200 employees was selected to participate in a new employee orientation survey. The results of the responses of the two groups were compared and were found to vary so much that the survey might have been made in two different companies. Foremen felt they had done a great job in orienting new employees, while new employees pointed out glaring deficiencies—particularly in units of high turnover. This came as no surprise. The survey questions follow.

	Foreman	*Employee*
1.	How much time did you spend in orienting new employees?	How much time did your foreman spend in telling you about your job and the company?
	a. 15 minutes or less.	a. 15 minutes or less.
	b. 30 minutes.	b. 30 minutes.
	c. 1 hour.	c. 1 hour.
	d. More than an hour.	d. More than an hour.
2.	Which subjects did you cover when orienting new employees during their first day of work?	Which subjects did the foreman talk about during your first day on the job?
	a. Pay procedures.	a. Pay procedures.
	b. Safety rules.	b. Safety rules.
	c. Parking lot assignment.	c. Parking lot assignment.
	d. Insurance plan.	d. Insurance plan.
	e. Cafeteria facilities.	e. Cafeteria facilities.
	f. Break and washup time.	f. Break and washup time.
	g. Medical facilities.	g. Medical facilities.
	h. Attendance.	h. Attendance.
	i. Vacations.	i. Vacations.
	j. Wage assignments.	j. Wage assignments.
	k. Profit-sharing plan.	k. Profit-sharing plan.
	l. Shop rules.	l. Shop rules.
	m. Tool check system.	m. Tool check system.
3.	How does the new employee learn what his job means in relation to the end product?	How did you learn what your job has to do with the final product?
	a. I take the employee to various areas.	a. The foreman took me on a quick tour and showed me.
	b. The employee never finds out.	b. I don't know what my job has to do with the end product.
	c. Other employees tell him.	c. Other employees told me.
	d. He takes a tour on his own.	d. By taking a plant tour by myself.

	Foreman	*Employee*
4.	If you did not spend much time on orientation, it was probably because	If the foreman did not spend much time on going over things with you, it was probably because
	a. You couldn't communicate with the employee.	a. He did not understand what you were saying.
	b. You had more pressing things to do.	b. He had to do more important things.
	c. The employee wasn't interested.	c. He didn't care.
	d. You couldn't find the time.	d. He didn't have time.
5.	How does a new employee meet his co-workers?	How did you meet your co-workers?
	a. I introduce him around.	a. The foreman introduced me.
	b. He meets them on his own.	b. I met them on my own.
	c. He never meets them.	c. I never met them.
6.	Do employees come to you with their questions and problems?	Will you go to the foreman with your questions and problems?
	a. Yes.	a. Yes.
	b. No.	b. No.
	c. Maybe.	c. Maybe.
7.	What have you instructed the employees to do if someone is seriously injured?	What would you do if the person next to you were seriously injured?
	a. Call the foreman.	a. Call the foreman.
	b. Nothing.	b. Nothing.
	c. Take him to the plant nurse.	c. Take him to the plant nurse.
	d. The subject never came up.	d. The subject was never brought up.
8.	How did your new employees learn they are on probation and exactly what that means?	How did you learn what it means to be a probationary employee?
	a. Personnel told them.	a. Personnel told me.
	b. I talked about this during their first week at work.	b. My foreman told me.
	c. Not sure they know.	c. I don't know what it means.
	d. Fellow employee probably told them.	d. Fellow employees filled me in.

	Foreman	*Employee*
9.	What have you instructed your new employees to do if they will be tardy or absent?	What do you do if you will be tardy or absent?
	a. Call personnel.	a. Call personnel.
	b. Nothing.	b. Nothing.
	c. Call the foreman direct.	c. Call the foreman and tell him.
	d. Call a fellow employee and let him tell the foreman.	d. Call a fellow employee and let him tell the foreman.
10.	What is the foreman's *main* job?	What is the foreman's *main* job?
	a. Getting parts and raw materials to the proper work stations.	a. Getting parts and raw material to the proper work stations.
	b. Helping and directing employees.	b. Helping and directing employees.
	c. Keeping production going.	c. Keeping production going.
	d. Keeping records up to date.	d. Keeping records up to date.
11.	How much on-the-job training do your new employees require?	How much on-the-job training did you need on your first job?
	a. Up to one day.	a. Up to one day.
	b. About one week.	b. About one week.
	c. Up to two hours.	c. Up to two hours.
	d. Two weeks or more.	d. Two weeks or more.
12.	During his first day on the job, what do you think the new employee was most concerned with?	During your first day on the job, what was your major concern?
	a. Getting along with fellow employees.	a. Getting along with fellow employees.
	b. Learning his job.	b. Learning the job.
	c. Not making any mistakes.	c. Not making any mistakes.
	d. Keeping up with other employees.	d. Keeping up with other employees.
13.	How do you check on the progress of new employees?	How does the foreman check on your progress on the job?
	a. By periodically checking their work.	a. By coming over and watching me work.

	Foreman	*Employee*
	b. Through reports from the utility and relief man.	b. Through reports from the utility and relief man.
	c. Do not check.	c. Does not appear to check.
	d. By speaking with them during breaks.	d. By speaking with me during breaks.
14.	If an employee feels that he is not being paid enough, which course of action do you instruct him to take?	If you felt that you were not being paid enough, what would you do?
	a. Quit work.	a. Quit work.
	b. Complain to the foreman.	b. Complain to the foreman.
	c. File a grievance.	c. File a grievance.
	d. Do nothing.	d. Nothing.
15.	If an employee asked about holiday pay, would you	If you asked a foreman about holiday pay, would you expect him to
	a. Answer the question yourself or tell him you'll get the answer?	a. Answer the question or say he'll find the answer?
	b. Refer him to someone who could answer him?	b. Refer you to someone who knew the answer?
	c. Tell him to read the booklets he received from personnel?	c. Tell you to read the personnel booklets?
	d. Ignore him?	d. Ignore the question?
16.	What characteristic of a new employee impresses you when you first meet?	What do you think the foreman looks for most in a new employee?
	a. Being well dressed.	a. Being well dressed.
	b. Learning speed.	b. Learning speed.
	c. Attentiveness.	c. Attentiveness.
	d. Positive attitude toward work.	d. Positive attitude toward work.
17.	What do you think happens to the booklets on benefits, shop rules, and so on that new employees receive from personnel?	What do you do with the booklets on benefits and wages you receive from personnel?
	a. The employee throws them away.	a. I throw them away.
	b. The employee keeps them but never refers to them.	b. I keep them but never refer to them.

	Foreman	*Employee*
	c. The employee keeps them and uses them to answer his questions.	c. I keep them to answer my questions.
	d. No idea.	d. I don't know.
18.	When you talk with new employees for the first time, what point do you stress?	When your foreman spoke with you for the first time, what did he stress?
	a. Neat attire.	a. Neat attire.
	b. Good attendance.	b. Good attendance.
	c. Safety rules.	c. Safety rules.
	d. Quality workmanship.	d. Quality workmanship.
19.	When you talk about overtime with new employees, how do you encourage them?	When your foreman talks to you about working overtime, what reasons does he give?
	a. Overtime is mandatory.	a. No choice; have to work overtime.
	b. It is a chance to earn extra money.	b. It is a chance to earn extra money.
	c. The work has to be done.	c. The work has to be done.
	d. By a team effort we can help one another.	d. By a team effort we can help one another.
20.	What would you do if you saw a new employee breaking a minor shop rule?	What would you expect the foreman to do if he saw you breaking a minor shop rule?
	a. Discharge him.	a. Discharge me.
	b. Take him aside and set him straight.	b. Take me aside and set me straight.
	c. Ignore it.	c. Nothing.
	d. Can't say; depends on the circumstances.	d. Don't know; I guess it would depend on the circumstances.
21.	How can we improve the process of introducing the new employee to his job? Explain.	How can we improve our methods of explaining the things that affect you on your job? Explain.
22.	What do you expect from a new employee?	What do you want from your job?

One-Day Induction Program

The orientation and induction survey clearly pointed out the need for a complete overhaul in the method of inducting new employees.

Because people are most likely to establish close ties with their peers, and because they may be more inclined to stay on a job where they are among friends, it was decided to use senior employees in the role of counselor–trainers. Each foreman was asked by the human resources executive to select two or more longer-service employees with the ability, experience, and desire to help coach teams of new employees in their job responsibilities and to see that they got off on the right foot.

The role of the counselor was to supplement and assist busy foremen as an interim step in making each new man feel comfortable and productive as soon as possible. It was recognized, partially because of the orientation and induction survey, that moving into this particular factory environment was a big adjustment for any individual. And it was during the early impressionable period that the new employee shaped his attitude toward the company and decided to quit or to stay.

Each foreman worked out with his counselors the specific training responsibilities he wanted them to assume. The counselors were given formal recognition, status, and extra pay for their efforts.

To get the employee favorably tuned in to the company, counselor–trainers needed to know how to apply (1) techniques of induction, (2) on-the-job training, (3) techniques of effective presentation, or communication skills. Classroom sessions were arranged to acquaint counselor–trainers with their new responsibilities. Seminars were also attended by foremen and manufacturing managers. The human resources executive led the discussions.

The classes consisted of three 3-hour sessions with provision for follow-up, audit, and measurement of individual counselor effectiveness in applying the lessons learned. The first session dealt with the job induction phase, which helped counselor–trainers understand the need to make the new employee interested in learning his job and aware of the importance of his work and the significance of his personal contribution to company and department goals. To this was added necessary information about the company, the type of work that new employees would be doing, and the problems of adjustment to the work group. Role-playing situations and case studies were developed by the human resources executive and used extensively to get students to share experiences.

The second session, the job instruction training phase, focused on teaching the skills that employees required in order to become efficient workers. The theory and application of on-the-job training were stressed along with an explanation of the incentive system and the pay plan.

The third session was the effective presentation phase, designed to sharpen communication skills of counselor–trainers in order to cultivate proper work attitudes and habits. The entire program was given a dry run and critiqued by both participants and management.

Provision was made to follow up and measure changes in absenteeism, tardiness, turnover, scrap and rework, grievances, safety, employee suggestions, financial responsibility, and productivity of new employees. Experimental and control groups were set up.

The results were astounding. There was significant improvement noted in every measure of the effectiveness of the approach, whether comparing a unit's past performance with present performance or comparing different units with each other. As a result, the approach was adopted in all departments.

The one-day job induction approach is summarized as follows:

Job Induction Program

WHEN AND WHERE	WHAT AND HOW	BY WHOM
1. On arrival to Personnel Office (7:30 A.M.)	1. *Information given on day's events:* a. Purpose of one-day induction b. Plant tour c. Role of counselor/trainer/foreman d. Transportation to and from work e. Starting time, coffee breaks, lunch period, washup and quitting time f. Opportunity for questions	1. Human Resources Representative
2. Group discussion (8:00 A.M.)	2. *Plant safety* a. Parking rules b. Security regulations	2. Safety Specialist
3. On arrival to appropriate product department (9:00 A.M.)	3. *Meeting supervisor, trainer, getting to know layout of building* a. Tour through plant, with general explanation of products methods, sequence of operations,	3. Departmental Counselor

Job Induction Program (Continued)

WHEN AND WHERE	WHAT AND HOW	BY WHOM
	work areas, and tools/equipment storage b. Show him where he is to work and have him meet foreman/trainer c. Show him lockers, washroom, employee store, parking lot, etc. d. Show him the timeclock and explain regulations e. Tell him about safety, dispensary services, and other special rules (smoking, leaving plant, etc.) f. Stress importance of teamwork, quality, and quality products	
4. Following No. 3 till 11:00 A.M.	4. *General orientation* a. Departmental organization and names/functions of key groups b. Suggestion/grievance system c. Pay system/incentives/overtime d. Educational opportunities/training program e. Planned advancement program f. Attendance (notification of absence)	

Job Induction Program (Continued)

WHEN AND WHERE	WHAT AND HOW	BY WHOM
	g. Housekeeping h. Safety practices i. Personal conduct/departmental policies	
5. 11:30 to noon	5. *Show location of cafeteria and eat lunch with new employees* a. Discuss recreation activities b. Opportunity to ask questions c. Handouts on miscellaneous information	
6. After lunch until half-hour before quitting time	6. *Job instruction training* a. Introduction to neighboring workers b. Prepare the employee c. Explanation d. Demonstration e. Trial performance by employee f. Job-habit fixation	6. Trainer
7. Half-hour before quitting time	7. *Assign lockers, explain washup procedure and work clothes needed*	7. Supervisor/Trainer

Looking to the Future

With the success of the one-day induction, a plan was established for future implementation should the business continue its rapid and explosive growth. If it should want to hire hundreds of new employees, mostly blacks, from the labor market, it would have to do so systematically. The approach called for one full week in a separate training facility. This *employment entry approach* was visualized as follows. The program (see Exhibit 8-2) would be administered by a project director and a behavioral research practitioner, on a flexible, fluid basis, depending on the individual and collective needs of participants. For

Exhibit 8-2.
EMPLOYMENT ENTRY PROGRAM SCHEDULE MONDAY THROUGH FRIDAY—WORK AND STUDY 7:30 A.M.–4:00 P.M.

MONDAY	TUESDAY	WEDNESDAY	THURSDAY	FRIDAY
Project Director Welcome Outline of week's events Introduction of staff Expectations High attendance Productivity Quality *Job Instructor* Attendance Reporting in Plant tour Foreman introductions The local union *Work Session* Use of hand tools *Medical Director* Use of medical facilities *Job Instructor* Assembly and disassembly of appliances *Employment Specialist* Educational opportunities Planned advancement Shop rules Your pay check *Job Instructor* Quiz	*Job Instructor* Quality standard Demonstration Inspection Performance Use of hand tools Role-playing situation A dissatisfied customer Employee sales The employee store Major appliances Perform assembly operations Riveting Punch press Wiring Air tools Handling and transporting Assembly and disassembly of appliances *Personnel Manager* Suggestion system A probationary employee Case study on violation of shop rules Slide program on managing money *Job Instructor* Quiz	*Methods and Time Standards engineer* Define and demonstrate production standards *Job Instructor* Role-play situation: The foreman's bad day Component assembly Spot weld Small parts Unit assembly Tapping Forming Machine (light) operations *Personnel Manager* Safety and good housekeeping Shop rules or standards of good conduct Transfers Job shift changes Union contract *Job Instructor* Assembly and disassembly of appliances Initiative—if you run out of work Quiz	*Job Instructor* Demonstrate and check use of materials and tools Conservation of production supplies Methods of parts fabrication Small- and medium-press work Brake forming Shearing Sanding *Personnel Counselor* Plant tour Problem-solving procedures Your foreman The local union Employee information Newsletter Mailings to the home Foreman and general management meetings *Job Instructor* Assembly and disassembly of appliances Quiz	*Job Instructor* Responsibility for machinery and equipment costs Demonstration Inspection Finishing: Use of hand paint spray units *Personnel Manager* Case study: employee reports to work drunk and tardy Slide program Benefits review Savings plan Insurance plan Pension Vacations Beneficiary *Job Instructor* Packaging and crating units and service parts *Training Specialist* Personnel manager Educational opportunities In-plant high school Planned advancement Scholarships The incentive pay system Wage administration—progression Your pay check *Job Instructor* Quiz

example, present knowledge of learning and development of attitudes of responsibility (which is admittedly somewhat limited) suggests that the ideal class size may well be 30 to 40 trainees. The organization to develop, mold, and change attitudes, as well as teach physical skills, is depicted in Exhibit 8-3.

It should be emphasized that the curriculum is not fixed or rigid. Although the tentative program could eventually accommodate 40 to 50 trainees per 40-hour week, meeting daily from 7:30 A.M. to 4:00 P.M., initial class size could be 10 to 15 to insure proper selection and development of job instructors.

Inasmuch as well over 90 percent of the trainees would be from underprivileged minority groups housed in ghetto areas near the plant, two or three job instructors should be minority group members, upgraded from the hourly ranks. This should help the company to develop responsible first-line supervisors and other exempt manufacturing personnel who relate well to hourly employees. More than half of the company's factory personnel are minority group members.

The labor market consists primarily of new entrants from predominantly nonwhite ghetto areas. Heavy hiring expenses have indicated that these people lack preparation for a career in industry. No sense

Exhibit 8-3.
ORGANIZATION CHART: EMPLOYMENT ENTRY PROGRAM

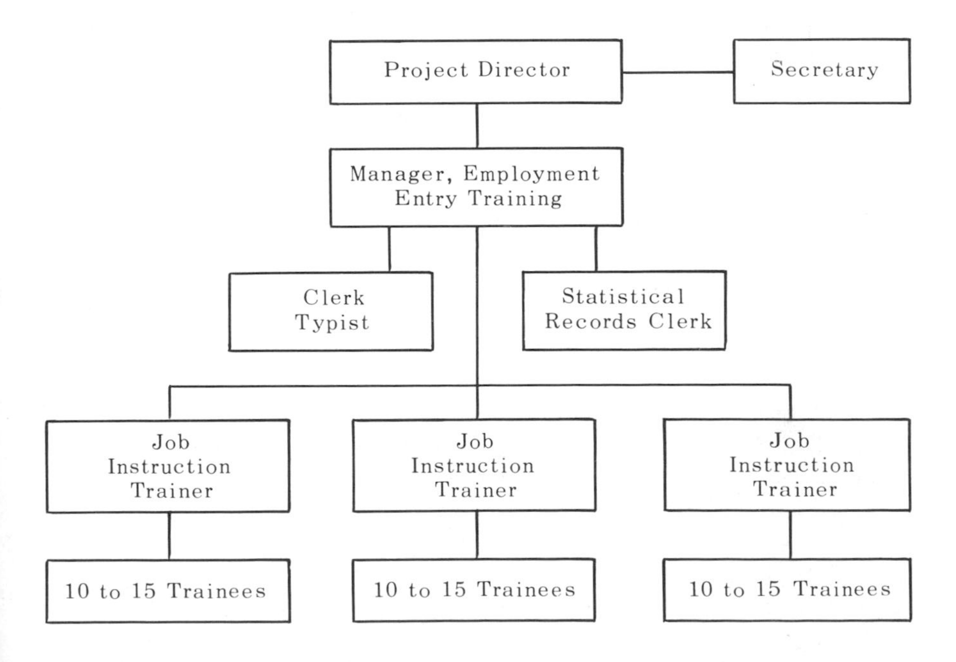

of responsibility had been imparted through home, school, church, or other institution.

An extensive preemployment testing program, which was not used as a screening device, convinced the company that the problem could be an attitudinal one because standardized, validated, and reliable verbal, nonverbal, dexterity, coordination, and precision tests failed to predict job performance or stayability. Before the one-day induction program was instituted, annual turnover skyrocketed from 30 to 80 percent. Absenteeism reached 15 percent in certain areas at given times; it was so bad that large numbers of people had to be sent home because closed-loop assembly lines could not operate with the remaining staff. Traditional approaches had to be discarded because existing communication systems and techniques proved ineffective in a production-oriented situation. Thus the employment entry program and curriculum were conceived and designed as a bridge to industrial life.

It should be reemphasized that this is a pioneering effort into an area where no existing knowledge is applicable; the emphasis is on attitudinal preparation coupled with appropriate skills learning.

As a beginning, it is anticipated that approximately half of participants' time will be spent in the classroom and half on skills training. Even in the skills area, however, attitudinal preparation will be stressed. Standard, previously successful learning and teaching techniques would be included; audiovisual materials, role playing and case studies, and other forms of group dynamics would be used extensively. The gap between the training facility and the shop would be bridged by plant tours and discussions as well as actual installation of a small productive line and fabrication center.

The project director would be free to experiment with the curriculum, time and length of sessions, media, and measurements as progress or the lack of it became evident. Initial plans would be to graduate about a thousand trainees annually for direct placement into factory positions.

It is assumed that favorable attitudes can be translated into higher productivity, improved quality, and other familiar quantitative measures. Therefore, experimental groups—designated as trainee groups—would be given positive support and immediate feedback of results. Control groups, hired at the same time from the same labor market using the same selection techniques, would be placed directly on open factory jobs in the traditional manner. Thus the effects of the program, if any, would become apparent in a matter of weeks.

Foremen, business section counselors, and job instructor trainers would be carefully selected and briefed both in the training facility and in the shop to insure the development of favorable shop climate and a smooth transaction with minimal problems of adjustment for trainees assigned to full-time jobs after completion of the employment entry program.

The objectives of the employment entry program can be summarized as follows:

1. To devise methods, techniques, and systems of measuring attitudes toward job, supervisor, company, self, and society and of measuring attitudinal change, changes in value systems, and preparation for handling a responsible factory job in a mass-production operation.
2. To prepare new entrants into the labor market from underprivileged minority groups to assume responsible factory jobs by providing attitudinal training to insure realization of personal goals through realization of corporate goals and objectives.
3. To reduce controllable factory employee turnover.
4. To reduce controllable factory employee absenteeism. (Controllable absenteeism is defined as absenteeism reported by employees as personal illness, personal business or illness in family or simply not reported.)
5. To reduce minimum, identifiable makeup and training costs.
6. To reduce total manufacturing variances.
7. To teach operations so that employees will be producing 100 percent of standard by the fifth day of training.
8. To teach new employees to correctly identify parts and their functions in finished, assembled kitchen appliances.
9. To make new employees aware of the costs of scrap and rework and their effect on job security as measured by (a) a daily quiz covering lecture materials which define and demonstrate product service costs, competitive pricing, costs of individual parts; (b) class discussion, role playing, and case studies to demonstrate customer reaction to poor quality.
10. To develop a recognition and acceptance of the team concept as a factor in achieving personal goals and objectives in life. Measure this recognition and acceptance by devising situations in the classroom and on the job to show class members that it is impossible to complete certain jobs and projects without team effort.
11. To teach the major provisions of the orientation program including benefits, shop rules, reporting absences and injuries, and so on. Measure by daily quiz on subjects covered in class. To teach employees the necessity for quality workmanship and how to achieve quality and recognize defective parts; set up quality control and inspection procedures to detect quality defects.

What About the Clerical Employee?

Many of the human resource considerations mentioned up to this point also have direct applicability to the group generally known as nonexempt, salaried employees. This group has grown vastly in numbers, and the special needs of its members do deserve special consideration. Two major areas are considered: performance appraisal and planned advancement.

The actual techniques for recording, evaluating, and discussing employee performance should closely parallel those that have been illustrated. But there are differences because this group does not have direct stewardship responsibility for managing company resources. While clerical employees should participate in goal setting, the degree to which they should be permitted to set their own performance standards is necessarily limited. Yet management must depend on this group to keep the business going, to help realize profit goals, to reduce costs, and to move up into positions of responsibility in lower and middle management. Discussion of individual performance results is equally important. The manager will have to pick up and carry the ball more frequently, but should encourage the individual to participate in the discussion and freely express his viewpoint.

The format for appraisal of a nonexempt salaried employee's performance is necessarily less complex than the one used for exempt salaried employees. The nonexempt format is shown in Exhibit 8-4.

Because most clerical employees are interested in advancement, opportunities must be made available to them. The best way to start is with a formal job description and a sound, competitive salary structure that has step rates or rate ranges for each grade and is well administered, updated, and communicated to all clerical employees. To get maximum mileage from these efforts, a planned advancement procedure should be initiated and communicated to all clerical employees in small groups called together by their immediate supervisors.

Simplicity and flexibility in administration are the best guidelines. A suggested procedure for planned advancement which encourages superviors and managers to meet with their people and assist in their advancement is incorporated in the following statement from management to clerical employees.

> One of the company's policies is to promote from within whenever qualified employees are available for consideration to positions with more responsibility and hence more pay.
>
> In order to implement this policy and utilize the full potential and talents of our clerical employees, a program of planned advancement is being initiated.

Exhibit 8-4.
PERFORMANCE RECORD FOR CLERICAL SALARIED EMPLOYEES

Employee's name________	Appraisal made by________	Date______
Function________	Reviewed by________	Date______
Position title________	Date discussed with employee________	
Grade (if applicable)________	Appraisal period: From______	To______
Date assigned to position______	Employee's signature________	

1. Knowledge of work gained through experience, general education, and specialized training.
   - ☐ Knowledge accumulation less than expected
   - ☐ Continued improvement with coaching
   - ☐ Knowledge evidences good training and experience
   - ☐ Thorough knowledge of all phases of work

   Comments:

2. Ability to plan work and go ahead with a job without being told every detail; ability to make constructive suggestions.
   - ☐ Work is unsystematic; evidences lack of initiative and/or planning
   - ☐ Progressing satisfactorily with guidance
   - ☐ Plans work well; develops assignments well
   - ☐ Consistently constructive and creative; unusually resourceful

   Comments:

3. Quantity of work accomplished in a given period of time.
   - ☐ Volume of work fails to meet expectations or standards
   - ☐ Volume gradually increasing
   - ☐ Volume acceptable to above average
   - ☐ Extraordinary speed; volume consistently high

   Comments:

4. Accuracy, thoroughness, and dependability of results—ability to turn out work which meets quality standards.
   - ☐ Makes too many mistakes; work requires constant checking; undependable
   - ☐ Gradually improving
   - ☐ Makes a few mistakes; aims for greater accuracy
   - ☐ Exceptional accuracy and dependability

   Comments:

5. Ability to do other work and adjust to new conditions.
   - ☐ Evidences inability to adjust to new situations; desire lacking
   - ☐ Readily grasps instruction; strong desire to learn
   - ☐ Reasonably satisfactory on new or different jobs; efficient
   - ☐ Highly adaptable and industrious; can be used on various jobs

   Comments:

Exhibit 8-4. (Continued)
PERFORMANCE RECORD FOR CLERICAL SALARIED EMPLOYEES

6. Success in integrating work effectively with others.
   - ☐ Experiences difficulties in interpersonal relations; uncooperative
   - ☐ Possesses favorable attitude toward others
   - ☐ Works well with others
   - ☐ Develops excellent cooperation from personnel not responsible to him

   Comments:

7. Attention to work, regularity of attendance, punctuality, response to schedule variations.
   - ☐ Sense of urgency is lacking; punctuality and/or attendance needs improvement
   - ☐ Aware of importance of regular attendance and proper notification of absence
   - ☐ Rarely neglects work; generally punctual; occasionally unable to meet schedule variations
   - ☐ Loses no time unnecessarily on job; rarely absent or late

   Comments:

8. What did the employee achieve during the appraisal period? Consider financial results where applicable, projects assigned, new ideas, methods and techniques proposed and adopted, cost improvements, etc. Give details. Include areas of underachievement as applicable. ____________________

   ____

9. Did any significant work obstacles develop during the appraisal period? What is being done to remove them? ____________________

   ____

10. Describe employee's strongest job-related assets. ____________________

    ____

11. Describe employee's job-related shortcomings. ____________________

    ____

12. Is this employee properly placed? Explain. ____________________

    ____

13. Does this employee evidence potential for promotion? ____________________
    To what positions? ____________________
14. Describe the plan you and the employee have developed to improve performance, remove obstacles to advancement, and insure continuing progress.

    ____

    ____

15. This final portion of the appraisal is a composite evaluation of performance based on level of contribution as defined in items 1 through 9. Please check appropriate blocks.
    - ☐ Unsatisfactory
    - ☐ Marginal
    - ☐ Satisfactory on most counts
    - ☐ Fully satisfactory
    - ☐ Superior
    - ☐ Outstanding

Exhibit 8-5.
PLANNED ADVANCEMENT REGISTER FOR CLERICAL SALARIED EMPLOYEES

Employee's name__________ Birth date__________

Date hired__________ Present position__________

Function__________ Present salary grade__________

Department__________ Date assigned to present position__________

Education

Circle highest grade completed 9 10 11 12 13 14 15 16 17 18

Name and location of high school__________

Dates attended__________

Name and location of college__________

Dates attended__________ Degree__________ Major__________

Other education (trade, vocational, secretarial, clerical, data processing)

Name and location of institution__________

Dates attended__________

Courses of study__________

Any physical limitations or handicaps? Yes ☐ No ☐

Describe__________

Employment history (starting with current position)

Dates				
From	To	Position	Company and location	Major duties
1.				
2.				

Type of position desired

Describe in detail positions you want to be considered for.

1. __________

2. __________

Employee's signature__________ Date__________

Supervisor's signature__________ Date__________

FOR USE OF PERSONNEL OFFICE ONLY

One of the purposes of this program is to insure that all clerical employees are afforded the oportunity to express their interest in advancement. Accordingly, you are asked to complete the attached planned advancement register form (Exhibit 8-5) if you wish to be considered for advancement. As you know, promotions are based on employee interest, attitude, motivation, stability, attendance, education, experience, and performance. The more information you can provide for the Register, the more you will enhance your chances for promotion.

All clerical salaried employees may complete planned advancement register application forms. Applications for upward, lateral, or downward moves will be accepted.

The new planned advancement program will operate as follows:

- Employee who wants to be considered for possible transfer will obtain a form from the supervisor and complete in detail.
- Supervisor will review, sign, and forward completed form to the personnel office via the supervising functional manager.
- The personnel office will develop a skills inventory from forms submitted.
- As requests for clerical salaried help are received by the personnel office, planned advancement register forms will be reviewed for capable candidates.
- The personnel office will arrange interviews with the supervisor who has the opening. The supervisor will notify the personnel office of his decision; if it is in the affirmative, the personnel office will make arrangements for transfer with the releasing supervisor.
- An employee whose qualifications change should notify the personnel office and the supervisor in writing to reflect these changes in the planned advancement register. Such changes include additional education, experience, special or temporary assignments, and outside related activities.

If you have any questions about the attached form or how this procedure will operate, please see your supervisor or arrange an interview with the human resources executive.

* * *

This chapter has presented a few selected examples of good human resource management in the hope that the problems of the factories and the offices will *not* be slighted by the human resources executive in his innovative problem-solving, opportunity-creating role. It is up to him to develop a balanced approach to human resource considerations at all organizational levels and for varying business conditions, both favorable and adverse. Neglect of human asset utilization at any level in any organization will have dire consequences and will eventually impair an organization's ability to achieve its goals.

9

A New Role in Business Effectiveness

The human resources executive now emerges as an internal consultant—a business effectiveness agent for purposeful and progressive change. His background of training and development point to a generalist's orientation as contrasted with the more narrowly focused point of view of a specialist.

Modern management at top organizational levels is beginning to recognize the need for high-level staff help in the solution of corporate problems—a great many of which can be traced to deficiencies in human resource management. Thus, though the staff role of the human resources executive used to be restricted to policy formulation and routine, traditional personnel activities, general management now looks to him to take an active role in stimulating change. His role as passive onlooker is a thing of the past.

The modern personnel director has enlarged the scope, responsibility, and context of his position to include all professional, administrative, managerial, scientific, and technical personnel as well as hourly, union, and clerical employees. His role as the new internal consultant can be well justified when an organization becomes so large and so complex that the policy group cannot alone control all major facets of the business. His catalytic role as a change agent puts him in a position where he has to be a good listener, an encourager of new ideas, a problem definer and innovator in his own right. He must suggest, review, and mediate solutions to problems, processes, or procedures. He stimulates organizational and individual behavior while developing or helping to foster a creative environment. He provides moral, physical, and psychological support to managers experimenting with change, encourages reasonable suggestions and the establishment of short-range organizational goals; he vetoes ineffective procedures and regularly reports progress toward goal attainment.

He is highly sensitive to people problems. He helps others to understand these problems by defining them more precisely. He assists in placing proper priorities on problems and giving consideration to a variety of possible solutions. He convinces management that decisions determined by consensus are insured the necessary supportive action. He literally initiates change and follows through to implementation.

Where Are the Pitfalls?

If the human resources executive appears to have a clearly defined role, why is it that so many companies fail to blend staff and line efforts to reach a common objective? Many an organization that is about to achieve a major breakthrough in technology or human relations fails to translate knowledge into action or results from staff to line.

Because modern management procedures have brought staff people into more direct contact with the traditional roles of line managers, both plans and results require a much closer working relationship. No doubt this trend will accelerate. It should be recognized, but often is not, that no matter how potentially valuable a management tool—be it long-range planning or managing by objectives—it is useless if the staff man fails to adapt his approaches to the needs of the line man or if the line manager is unwilling or unable to use the staff man's input.

From the standpoint of the line manager, the bright staff man is a know-it-all who insists with a degree of arrogance that his approach is exactly what is needed to solve a problem, without regard for the realities of time and cost or for the reactions of employees when their norms and life style are infringed upon. As an example, a new graduate of a management training program proposed a solution to a chronic absenteeism problem that literally would have forced the plant to shut down. The facts were these. Every year at the start of the deer-hunting season absenteeism zoomed. Management had long since become reconciled to this unofficial community holiday without pay. But the staff man, ignoring local custom, chose to regard this as a flouting of work rules and urged that penalties be meted out to all absentees. (The union contract had never been invoked on this issue.) Had his proposal been adopted, work would have been brought to a halt by a wildcat strike. The company would have been better advised to make the annual event an official holiday without pay.

Another frequent and related complaint of line people is that the staff man, with his strong sense of mission, makes a proposal that has a sound theoretical basis, but is totally inappropriate to his urgency and priorities. Here is a case in point. A young man from the human resources executive's staff once approached a vice president of manufacturing who was working with his foremen to install a standard cost system. The staff man from the corporate office wanted to talk about key replacement planning and management development. But the manufacturing man needed help in teaching his foremen practical applications of standard cost analysis. Thus the human resources representative missed the boat in failing to recognize and meet the manager's real needs to provide a basis for future acceptance of corporate staff ideas.

Other examples are pressuring a division manager to get his long-range plan in on time when he has a major quality problem to resolve or trying to impose a formal performance appraisal system on a harassed line manager who is trying to avert a strike.

Too often, the internal consultant sees only the aspects of a particular situation that relate to his special interests. Thus, when he constructs a solution to the problem, he takes into account only a small portion of the factors in a particular situation. One organization succeeded in broadening its human resources executive's viewpoint by giving him responsibility for business planning and the integration of appropriate corporate staff knowledge, skills, and abilities. When he went out to visit with a division manager and his staff, his focus was not limited to executive manpower planning; he would arrange to have corporate staff representatives meet with their line management counterparts when the time came to put together an intermediate-range plan. In the process, a total corporate planning system evolved which was endorsed and supported by both line and staff personnel. This put an end to fragmented, partial solutions to problems, and it brought order to the visitation schedule and minimized disruptions in the workday of busy line managers.

On the other hand, line managers are given to tossing a problem to the staff consultant and expecting an immediate solution. Ideally, a decision is arrived at jointly by line and staff after free and open consultation. More typically, the human resources executive comes up with an idea—for example, analysis of profitability by product in order to evaluate each salesman's true contribution to business results—then finds that *he* is expected to do the job of obtaining a profitability analysis by item.

Thus the shifting emphasis on the use of staff consultants to produce significant improvement in the performance of line activities must be accepted and acted upon to maintain the consultant's credibility. Yet, if he doesn't understand the system and the key relationships, he cannot solve a problem and indeed may aggravate it. Witness the case of a consultant selling product distribution computer analysis to the marketing executive. If the marketing executive buys the analysis he is in for trouble unless he understands its potential impact on inventories, warehouse locations, retailers' needs, lead time, and factory schedules. A great deal more than just freight costs is involved.

Even when line managers appreciate the benefit of a technique—say, proper use of an operating committee—they may delegate the responsibility for obtaining results and then fail to follow up and implement the projects or ideas. For example, a division manager who had a problem in synchronizing the goals and activities of engineering, marketing, and manufacturing asked the human resources executive to help establish a product planning committee. At the first meeting, the human resources executive was left to run the meeting, despite his efforts to bounce the ball back to the division manager. The modus operandi was established; agenda priorities were defined, and a plan was evolved by the group to coordinate the departments' activities. But it took two subsequent meetings to get the division manager to approve action that he had previously agreed with. While he appreciated the technique, he was reluctant to delegate the operating authority necessary to implement recommendations.

Frequently, busy internal consultants shift their schedules and put in long hours to accommodate a line manager's call for help. After much preparation and careful scheduling, the consultant may find that he is receiving relatively little help or information from the manager or his people.

These problems of reluctance have some deeper implications. The line manager may be wary of the staff consultant's new tools and techniques because, to his way of thinking, the body of knowledge and experience on which he has built his career may no longer be adequate to the needs of the job; a weakness may be exposed; his career may crumble. It is not unusual for staff innovations to require the line manager to operate in new ways, as well as to think in new ways. So the behavior and empathy of the staff trainer are most important in bringing about behavior change in the line manager.

If the staff man masks his own uneasiness and anxiety with a stream of technical language, communication will be nonexistent. It should never be implied, for example, that the line manager has not been running his operations effectively or that the consequence of his failure to adopt recommendations can be his failure as a manager.

The staff consultant is oriented toward an analytical approach. He has a good bag of tricks and is eager to prove their worth. It is difficult for him to understand the line manager's preoccupation with things he regards as more important. When the consultant finds that his success hinges on the cooperation of unenthusiastic or downright hostile managers, he tends to overreact, push harder, argue more forcefully. In fact, human resources consultants, internal and external, have been known to make their points so forcefully that they killed the program or the assignment they were trying to put across.

Pathways to Improvements

An honest appraisal of an organization's shortcomings will in most instances reveal where actual achievements fall short of potential and why there are many disappointments. But to improve his total contribution the human resources executive should not undertake a project or assignment until the line manager is ready to contribute his inputs, until he is ready to invest his time despite his many pressures, until he is ready to accept the fact that an immediate payoff is not always possible. Readiness is important.

When the human resources executive is new to the position or to the manager, he should start with a project that has a high probability of success. For example, a market study initially would prove to be far more valuable to the division manager than an entire long-range plan with all of its intricacies and complexities.

The staff man must also be prepared to share project responsibility and control with the line manager, but not let him relinquish his role when the project is off the ground. Too often, short cuts get results but bypass line involvement, and the solutions prove to be costly in the long run.

Unless there are problems on the line requiring close surveillance and control, line managers should be free to decide for themselves whether to use the in-house staff man; having to foot the bill directly (apart from a general assessment) would make for some meaningful project work and closer cooperation.

Line people should avoid the excuse that they have no time for all those newfangled ideas because many of these ideas—the application of new approaches to human resources management, for example—depend for their success on the understanding and support of key line managers.

The human resources consultant, for his part, must avoid telling line managers what to do and learn instead to help them. The task of the teacher is not to see how much ground he can cover, but to uncover a little bit of ground. Coupled with this is the need to avoid overwhelming the line manager with a host of consultants, each called in for a different purpose. Staff people need to integrate their efforts to help busy line managers. They must understand the important trends and dynamics of the particular business or component in which they are working.

One effective technique to improve working relationships between line and staff is to switch jobs regularly at all levels. This arrangement is a great help in arresting executive obsolescence, rounding out key men, and strengthening the organization. It certainly helps to break down barriers between line and staff people; there's nothing like working on both sides of the fence to make them appreciate each other. Not only do the managers benefit, but so do the functions they manage. People learn to become more flexible, and the organization learns to change so that it can compete in a world of rapid change.

Those who have sat on both sides of the fence find many new and stimulating challenges. They learn to adapt quickly and to use both overall strategy and day-to-day operating tactics with equal proficiency. Most managers agree that the most important decisions they make are people decisions. The best perspective for such decisions is provided by exposure to both line and staff assignments. A staff man would not approach his job as an observer who uncovers problems if he had line experience. Instead, he would seek to build close working relationships before trying to solve problems.

One of the best vehicles for bringing line and staff people together is the planning process. All key line managers should be asked to identify where their operations are going three to five years in the future and to describe how they plan to get there. This immediately opens up areas of shared interest where the expertise of both line and staff can be blended to produce the results that are best for the company.

Another way to meld the efforts of line and staff is to devote a full day to a discussion of human asset management. The human resources executive should plan such a meeting in a way that would require participation of the company's top line and staff executives. He might do well to circulate in advance to all participants a few good recent articles on manager manpower planning and development. Best results are achieved when the meeting bears a direct relationship to a companywide effort to which all have subscribed. For example, a meeting on executive manpower planning could be related to a five-year projection of business growth and development. To achieve appropriate impact and bring the subject into focus, the president's introductory comments should stress everyone's expressed concern for the company's human asset management responsibility.

This could be followed up by having the personnel director project executive manpower attrition: resignations, terminations, deaths, and retirements. In addition, he should forecast managerial demands based solely on company growth and expansion. To cap off his presentation illustrating the need for action, he should cite census figures noting the expected decrease in population growth through 1977. If these figures were displayed beside the chart projecting company needs, it would become obvious that outside recruiting is not the answer to future manpower needs. Add to this the anticipated changes in organization, job content, products, markets technology, systems, and procedures—and it becomes clear that in-house training is mandatory.

The line and staff executives should be assigned specific questions for discussion. A panel of top line and staff people should raise key issues which would necessitate some real brainstorming to develop solutions and answers.

A top line manager could ask, for instance, "Is executive manpower planning really necessary?" or "How do we know whether we have all the talent we need for growth right within the company?" He might challenge each of the division managers to identify his ten best performers regardless of where they were in the organization. Or he might ask: "Isn't it enough to use good selection techniques at lower levels?" and "Are we making the best use of our executive talent at the present time?" The meeting participants could be expected to pinpoint the need to establish a manpower inventory and a system for identifying promotable people for intra-company mobility.

To trigger discussion, perhaps a staff man could say that the best beginning is to have top quality people in all key positions with a lot of potential for advancement. And someone from the panel might ask: "What does it take to bring in and hold top quality people, and are we equipped to do so?" Perhaps what is needed is a way to improve the performance of key people. This line of reasoning could lead to a consensus for using management by objectives. Certainly current practices involving performance standards, measuring individual results, cooperation, selection, and training—all would have to be explored and examined.

If the consensus seems to be that there are not enough backup people on board, cost is a major consideration. The cost of promoting the wrong person and having him turn in a mediocre performance must be balanced against the probable costs of mistakes in hiring or deteriorating morale. It will become evident that overreliance on outside hiring is as unsatisfactory a solution as keeping a marginal performer in a key position.

Another key line executive could ask how practical it is to make enough time available to do an adequate job in manpower planning and what precisely is involved. The freewheeling discussions that such questions stimulate should be taped, and the human resources executive should serve as a resource person—helping to stimulate discussion and response.

Eventually, the discussions should be guided to the point of consensus, conclusion, and recommendations. Each manager should come to see that he can use staff services in discharging one of his prime responsibilities—the preparation of a qualified replacement for himself—and insuring that each of his key people is similarly engaged. An action program should commence immediately, spearheaded by the company president and the human resources executive in response to the needs highlighted at the meeting. It is important that human resources management receive its impetus and its point of view from the needs of line managers. They will support whatever program is built around their own expressed needs.

Accent on Value

One of the human resources executive's most effective tools for cementing line and staff efforts into a coordinated, cooperative undertaking is the business effectiveness task force.

Often, in the course of time, a business is in need of renewal. People and processes get sluggish; the old zip is replaced by complacency; it becomes more difficult to make a fair profit because of rising costs, poor quality, low productivity, and a general lack of concern. To provide the needed renewal in such a situation the human resources executive can work with top management to spearhead a rally-round-the-flag competition designed to get as many employees as possible—line and staff, salaried and hourly—personally involved at all levels. People want to help and will respond if the venture has appeal and personal reward and if it is well organized and executed.

An overall unifying theme must come from the top policy-making group. A catchy title is likely to bring a good response—perhaps ONE GOAL—CUSTOMER SATISFACTION or OPERATION UPTURN or OPERATION RENEWAL. The theme, posters, publications, charts, and the rest can feature a boat race, a horse race, or a race around the world. Attractive, costly prizes should go to the winners. Departments should compete with one another according to a clearly stated plan to achieve a specified degree of profit improvement by reducing scrap and rework, improving shipments, or improving attendance, housekeeping, and safety.

The most senior managers should serve as judges, and a number of task force teams could be organized into functional or departmental groups; for example, engineering, marketing, manufacturing, controls, and personnel. Membership on any one task force should be composed of middle and lower management people, line and staff, who are not ordinarily assigned to work in that particular function, department, or area. The advantages of exposure, broadening, and objectivity are important here.

Progress should be reported formally every week and should be charted everywhere. There should be weekly prizes; cake and coffee to individual and group winners in every subcategory. Employee interest is heightened with a traveling plaque that is relocated weekly—and such displays as a hippopotamus, properly inscribed, for the worst attendance record and a beaver, also inscribed, for the best attendance record. These displays should be large and freestanding, and they should be placed outside the door of the appropriate department head at the beginning of the week. Winners for the greatest number of weeks could go to the Rosebowl—at company expense.

This is not an excuse for a cost reduction project; it is an opportunity to get everyone working harmoniously for a common cause. It may mean the survival of the business; it may mean the difference between growth and stagnation. It is an excellent developmental tool for young people with high potential; they could chair the task force groups weekly—elected by their fellow group members because of their personal contribution to the goals of the group.

The point is that, if the human resources executive is indeed to be an agent of business effectiveness, he himself must introduce change and encourage others to do likewise.

* * *

The human resources executive must take the lead role in building flexible, innovative problem-solving teamwork among responsible managers, supervisors, and individuals at all organizational levels. He must initiate activity that encourages people to work together willingly—to help management to get things done through people. As management develops expertise in participative leadership, as individuals identify their personal goals with operational objectives, as people anticipate, plan for, and meet future needs of the business, the process of learning, growing, and adapting becomes a way of life. Good habits begin to displace bad, problems come to be viewed as opportunities, and the organization comes up with exciting breakthrough alternatives.

An organization is built not by hiring more inspectors to catch rejects, but by incorporating quality into every facet of a manager's human relationships—from recruiting to utilizing to motivating to developing to compensating and, hence, to retaining his people. People considerations must become an integral part of every managerial decision from broad, overall strategic long-range planning to the tactical, day-to-day execution and implementation of active plans, policies, systems, and procedures.

The executive, using his tools of professional human relations knowledge and discipline along with his acute awareness of the nature and needs of the business, can exert a significant positive influence on the quality of human resource management—the real key to business success.

Appendix A
Professional Employees
Part 1: Effective Recruiting Tools

The Position Specification
The Man Specification
The Position Description
The Interview Evaluation Record
The Application Blank

POSITION SPECIFICATION: QUALITY CONTROL ENGINEER

Reports to: Manager–Quality Control
Department: Home Laundry
Section: Home Laundry Operation
Subsection: Quality Control

Broad Statement of Position Responsibilities:

Provide, through purchasing, technical support to vendors of home laundry parts and components. Provide detailed quality planning to meet engineering specifications on assigned purchased components, including design and/or specification of the necessary quality information equipment. Make disposition of rejected materials. Define quality standards, such as appearance, color, noise, not specified by product engineering.

Key Results Expected:

1. Effective technical support to purchasing, as measured by the percentage of incoming lots rejected.
2. Effective quality planning, as measured by purchased materials later rejected in process and the service call rate experienced in the laboratory and the field.
3. Effective dispositions of rejected lots of material that are timely and result in the lowest overall quality costs to the home laundry department.

Climate:

To be measured closely on results.

PERSONNEL REQUEST: QUALITY CONTROL ENGINEER

PERSONNEL REQUEST						DATE PREPARED March 31, 19—			
UNIT NAME Quality Control		SUB-SECTION Quality Control		SECTION Operations		DEPARTMENT Home Laundry			
TOTAL NO. REQD. 1	SEX M	NO. ADDITIONS	NO. REPLACEMENTS 1	DATE REQD. 6/7/—	LOC.—PLT. & BLDG. 1	BONDING YES X	BONDING NO	PAT. AGREE. YES X	PAT. AGREE. NO
1ST SHIFT	NUMBER	START TIME 8:30 AM	FINISH TIME 5:00 PM	X	EXEMPT SALARY		HOURLY INCENTIVE		
2ND SHIFT	NUMBER	START TIME	FINISH TIME		NONEXEMPT SALARY		HOURLY DAYWORK		
3RD SHIFT	NUMBER	START TIME	FINISH TIME	TO BE INTERVIEWED BY D. A. Ridyard					

SPECIFIC POSITION DUTIES—ONLY REQUIRED FOR SALARIED PERSONNEL
Initial assignment will be in Purchased Materials area. See position guide and organization chart attached. After one year, man should be capable of transfer to Factory Support area.

SPECIFIC EMPLOYEE REQUIREMENTS—AGE, EDUCATION (DEGREE OR MAJOR), AMT & TYPE OF EXPERIENCE, AND EQUIP. TO BE OPERATED
BSME or BS in other technical or engineering area, such as IE, EE, math, chemistry, physics; age 25 to 35; M.T.P. graduate or equivalent; work experience of 3 to 5 years.

See Position and Man Specifications attached.

	APPROVED	DATE	APPROVED	DATE

FOR UNIT NO.	POSITION TITLE	JOB/POS. NO.	GRADE/LEVEL	ACCOUNT NUMBER	
	Quality Control Engineer		L-8		

MAN SPECIFICATION: QUALITY CONTROL ENGINEER

Reports to: Manager–Quality Control
Department: Home Laundry
Section: Home Laundry Operation
Subsection: Quality Control

Education:
BSME, BSIE, BSEE, or BS in physics or math or in some other engineering discipline. Man should be from top 25% of his school class.

Experience:
Internal management training program graduate or equivalent; 3–5 years experience in manufacturing. Prefer experience in manufacturing engineering quality control. Experience in production engineering would also be excellent. Depth of knowledge or experience in quality control is not required.

Age: 25–35

Personal Attributes:
Must be mature and able to plan, organize, integrate, and measure his own work. Must be able to get results in dealing with others who are not responsible to his position. Above all, must be able to analyze data, situations, and problems to determine cause and effect and to make sound judgments and decisions based on facts.

POSITION DESCRIPTION: QUALITY CONTROL ENGINEER

Broad function: Provide the detailed quality control planning to meet engineering specifications for assigned products or areas. Determine that quality requirements have been completely defined and that product specifications are compatible with available manufacturing and quality measurement techniques.

Reports to: Manager–Quality Control

Principal Responsibilities

1. Establish detailed procedures for controlling the quality of materials, parts, components, subassemblies, and final product.
2. Designate material quality characteristics to be measured and their respective quality levels. Specify sampling plans, inspection, and test equipment to be used.
3. Develop plans for vendor materials, quality ratings, and materials quality certification by vendors.
4. Provide timely quality data and reports for quality-related decision making.
5. Participate with marketing and engineering in establishing and defining the quality standards which cover such items as appearance, color, noise, and vibration.

6. Review new and revised product designs for quality.
7. Analyze pilot runs, identify nature of problems and refer such problems to the appropriate function for action.
8. Recommend improvements to engineering and manufacturing to increase product uniformity and reliability and improve quality characteristics.
9. Determine quality capabilities required for machines, processes, and equipment.
10. Provide technical assistance and guidance to shop operations supervision for application of total quality system.

INTERVIEW EVALUATION RECORD

Name: ____________________ **Date:** __________ **Age:** ______

Job Considered for: ______________________________ Exempt ______

Nonexempt ______

Interviewer: ____________________

Summary Evaluation

Work Experience	+ Average −
Education	+ Average −
Early home background	+ Average −
Current off-job influences	+ Average −
Total	+ Average −

Referred by: ____________________
Disposition: ____________________
Referred to: ____________________
Action: ____________________

1. Work experience: | + | A | − |

Type, amount, relevance
Work conditions
Level of responsibility
Salary progression
Gains and contributions
Likes and dislikes
Problems
Current and future objectives

2. Education: | + | A | − |

Years and type
Major and minors
Best and poorest subjects
Scholastic level
Special achievements
Extracurricular activities
How financed
Future objectives

3. Early home background: | Satisfactory | Unsatisfactory |

Socioeconomic
Father's occupation
Number in family
Parental influence

4. Current off-job influences: | Strengths | Difficulties |

Marital status
Dependents
Financial
Activities and hobbies
Appearance, energy, health

5. Overall summary: | E | AA | A | BA | P |

E = Excellent
AA = Above Average
A = Average
BA = Below Average
P = Poor

Consider:

Appearance and personality
Abilities and skills
Motivations and interests
Impact as a person
Summary of technical qualifications

APPLICATION FOR SALARIED EMPLOYMENT

APPLICATION FOR EMPLOYMENT . . . *SALARIED*

(Please print or type all information)

Name ______________________________ Date ________
(LAST) (FIRST) (MIDDLE)

Address ______________________________ Phone ________
(NO. AND STREET) (CITY) (STATE) (ZIP)

Position desired ______________ Second choice ______________

Salary desired ________ Minimum acceptable ________ Date available ________

Birthplace ______________ Birth date ______________ Age ________

Are you a U.S. citizen? __ If not, give Alien Reg. No. __ Have lived in U.S. __ yrs

Married? ________ Number of children ________ Number of dependents ________

Physical disabilities ______ ______________ Height ______ Weight ________

Were you ever employed by this company? ___ If yes, when? ___ Your position ____

List names of relatives or friends employed by this company ______________

EDUCATION . . .

High school ______________________ No. years attended ________
(NAME)

Address ____
(CITY) (STATE)

Did you graduate? ________ Date _______ Scholastic record ______________

Honors ____
(PRIZES, SCHOLARSHIPS, HONORARY SOCIETIES, ETC.)

Activities ____
(ATHLETIC, DRAMATIC, EDITORIAL, ETC.)

____

____

College–University ______________________ Attended ______________
(NAME) (FROM) (TO)

Address ____
(CITY) (STATE)

Major field ______________ Degree received __________ Date ________

Minor field ______________ Academic record ______________
(% STANDING IN CLASS)

Honors ____
(PRIZES, SCHOLARSHIPS, HONORARY SOCIETIES, ETC.)

Activities ____
(ATHLETIC, DRAMATIC, EDITORIAL, ETC.)

List any additional schooling ______________________________

PROFESSIONAL ACTIVITIES . . .

Professional society memberships ______________________________

(LIST SOCIETIES, CLASS OF MEMBERSHIPS, DATES, COMMITTEE ACTIVITIES, ETC.)

____

____

Publications ______________________________

(LIST TITLES, PUBLICATION MEDIA, DATES OF PUBLICATION, ETC.)

____

Talks and addresses ______________________________

(LIST TITLES, SOCIETIES BEFORE WHICH PRESENTED)

____

Patents ______________________________

(STATE IN WHAT FIELDS)

____

Honors ______________________________

(LICENSES, LISTINGS IN DIRECTORIES, ETC.)

____

PERSONAL . . .

What were your objectives in selecting your field of study? ______________________________

____

____

What kind of work (individual contributor, specialist, managerial) do you seek in furthering your career ambitions? ______________________________

____

____

What position (level of management field) do you aspire to in the next 5 to 10 years for which you feel you are capable? ______________________________

____

____

What do you consider to be your areas of greatest strength (personal attributes, functional, professional, or managerial abilities)? ______________________________

____

____

What are your hobbies? ______________________________

List civic activities, memberships, participation, etc. ______________________________

____

Have you ever been arrested? (other than traffic violation) ____________ What was the charge? ______________________________

____

EMPLOYMENT HISTORY . . .

List most recent first

Company____________________ From______ To______

(DATES)

Address____________________ Salary________

(CITY) (STATE)

Nature of company's business____________________

Supervisor____________________ Your position________

(NAME AND TITLE) (TITLE)

Describe your duties____________________

____

Reason for leaving____________________

MILITARY HISTORY . . .

Branch of service____________________ From______ To______

(DATES)

Rank or rating at entry________ Rank or rating at separation________

Principal military duty____________________

Awards or citations____________________

Are you now a member of: Ready reserve?________ Standby reserve?________

When does service end?____________________

Selective Service Status: Classification____________ Until________

*Applicant's Signature*____________ *Soc. Security No.*________ *Date*________

DO NOT WRITE BELOW THIS LINE

Remarks:

Interviewed by:____________________ Date____________

Payroll No.____________________ Charge Account No.________

Starting date____________ as____________________

Department____________________ Position No.________

Salary______ Mo. ☐ W'k. ☐ Ex. ☐ Nonex. ☐ Salary grade or level______

Reporting to:____________________

Appendix A: Part 2 Representative Policies

Management Development
Educational Assistance
Tuition Refund

MANAGEMENT DEVELOPMENT POLICY

Policy

The future growth of the company depends in large measure on the continuing development of executive manpower. It is the policy of the company, therefore, to provide the environment and the opportunities to enable each individual to develop to the full extent of his potential, consistent with his needs, interests, abilities, and willingness to put forth extra effort to realize this potential.

Purpose

The purpose of this policy is to recognize and encourage development as an individual process involving the interaction of the man, his job, his manager and the work environment. The end result is to meet the company's future needs for competent managers from within the company through accelerating advancement of key potential individuals by identifying and utilizing strengths and eliminating or reducing shortcomings. Development implies positive changes in behavior, and hence, improvement in performance.

Approach

The management development process focuses attention on:

(a) Those conditions which have an important effect on the ability and the willingness of managers to perform. Such conditions include, for example: definition of position responsibilities, performance standards, appraisal systems, individual development programs, manpower inventories and replacement charts.

(b) Typical development activities, such as individual participation in goal-setting, coaching, counseling, feedback by managers and special job assignments for the individual as well as outside courses of study.

Responsibilities

The operating executive vice presidents, through their line management organizations, are responsible for insuring that the company policy of management development is fully and effectively implemented in all their operations.

The corporate staff is responsible for assisting operating management in developing and implementing appropriate programs within the division.

EDUCATIONAL ASSISTANCE POLICY

It is the company policy to provide financial assistance to salaried nonunion employees who undertake formal programs of study as part of their continuing development.

Purpose

The educational assistance program, including tuition refund, is designed to—

1. Encourage employees to fill specific job-related voids in their educational background through sources not available within the company.
2. Keep employees knowledgeable about the constantly changing technology in their functional disciplines.
3. Help prepare employees for advancement and thus provide future managers to meet the needs of our rapidly growing, changing business.

Responsibilities

1. The operating executive vice presidents, through their line management organizations, are responsible for insuring that the educational assistance policy is effectively implemented.
2. The corporate staff is responsible for assisting operating management in developing and implementing appropriate plans and monitoring their effectiveness.

TUITION REFUND POLICY

Purpose

In recognition of the increasing complexity of our business operations together with the need for our personnel to remain abreast of new developments in these areas, the tuition refund program provides managers a means whereby, at their discretion, they may reimburse an employee for part or all of the tuition costs for courses in which he voluntarily enrolls at the undergraduate or graduate level at a recognized college or university.

Objective

In keeping with this purpose, the tuition refund program is designed to meet the following objectives:

To encourage employees to fill specific voids or weaknesses in their educational background related to their work through sources which are not readily available within the company.

To provide a means whereby employees may remain knowledgeable of the constantly changing technology in their respective functional area. To help assure the company an adequate supply of qualified manpower to meet the changing needs of the business.

Eligibility

Managers may approve tuition refund payments to any full-time employee who undertakes a course or courses related to the employee's current job, or related to a job into which the manager feels the employee is promotable within the near future.

It is not intended that this program provide reimbursement for courses taken of a seminar or vocational nature, such as those offered by correspondence, trade, business or secretarial schools.

Policy

Enrollment must be in a college or university listed and fully accredited by one of the six regional accrediting associations. The course itself must give credit toward a degree, although the student may not necessarily be enrolled for the purpose of obtaining a degree. High school level courses will not be reimburseable under the tuition refund program.

Eligibility for reimbursement is dependent upon successful completion of the approved course. "Successful completion" is defined as meaning that the minimum grade accepted by the school for credit toward graduation has been obtained. The amount of allowable reimbursement will then be directly dependent upon the grade received. The following relationship will exist between grade received and reimbursement:

A—100% Tuition Costs
B— 75% Tuition Costs
C— 50% Tuition Costs

Tuition charges are considered to include only tuition, initial registration fees and laboratory fees. No other fees or charges are covered by the term "tuition."

Attendance by employees at courses and participation in this program must be at the initiative of the employee.

No tuition refunds will be made to employees whose employment with the company terminates prior to completion of the course. Exceptions will be cleared through the manager–executive development.

Employees currently receiving financial aid (fellowships, G.I. Bill, etc.) are not eligible to participate.

Responsibility

Reimbursement for tuition costs under this program requires that the employee obtain approval in advance of enrollment. The responsibility for approving participation in this program rests with the division manager, or those persons reporting to him to whom the authority for approval may be delegated.

The manager–executive development will have the responsibility to evaluate and interpret the policy as it relates to current needs; recommend appropriate revisions in the policy; and perform audits of the program application.

Appendix A: Part 3 Management Development—Examples

Key Replacement Planning
Early Identification
Position Description: Company President
Personnel Specifications: Company President—Candidate Qualification Analysis
Performance Appraisal and Review
Sample Manpower Inventory Form—Individual
Attitude Survey

INITIAL PLANNING FOR MANAGEMENT DEVELOPMENT

It is recommended that the initial management development effort be concentrated in two areas: key individual replacement planning and early identification of young executives with high potential.

Key Individual Replacement Planning

The initial thrust should include all senior management personnel on the current organization chart. The human resources executive should sit down with each individual on the chart commencing with the company president and cover five items:

1. Develop an up-to-date position description with each person for his position.
2. Develop a set of manpower specifications by discussing with the individual the pertinent qualifications needed to fill the position.
3. Have each individual nominate at least one and preferably two replacements for himself: an emergency replacement and a planned replacement to be available within two years. Each manager who names a replacement candidate must support his nomination by discussing the individual's quantitative and qualitative accomplishments. This includes a rating of present performance and a rating of promotability. The manager should then go back and discuss the individual's career interest with him to determine compatibility with the manager's thinking. When the manager rates the individual on promotability, he must be prepared to discuss specific developmental needs relative to the

position. Upon completion of the ratings of performance and promotability, the manager will forward the papers to the next two higher levels of management for review and approval.

4. Have each manager, in consultation with the human resources executive, develop a program for each of his key replacements to fill gaps in training and experience. The program should include—
   a. *On-the-job experience* such as job rotation, job enlargement, special assignments, task force participation, assignments as assistant-to, and on-the-job coaching and development.
   b. *Outside training* such as university programs, specific functional disciplines taught by management education consultants, and special courses such as sensitivity training. These would be directly geared to the individual's needs.
   c. Prepare *developmental timetables* for each manager's key replacements. Progress on these timetables should be reviewed periodically with the human resources executive.
5. If there is no potential replacement on board who can be ready within two years, the manager will be requested to hire an outside backup within one year. This backup will then be groomed according to a predetermined plan which will round out his qualifications and expertise. This replacement candidate should be added to the payroll or replace a key executive who is not fully measuring up to his position requirements.

Early Identification of Young Executives with High Potential

Each division manager and corporate staff head will be asked to identify at least three people on his staff, age 25 to 35 years, who have demonstrated by superior performance their potential for advancement to general management. This part of the initial management development effort should be initiated concurrently with the key individual replacement planning and works as follows.

The human resources executive will review with each division manager and corporate staff head his nominations of "high potentials," supported by a report of each individual's accomplishments on his present position. These reviews should be recorded on personnel evaluation forms.

Each nominee will be rated on both present performance and potential for advancement. Since many in the high-potential category will have had little or no formal management training, their development will include in-house training and out-of-house courses and seminars. This outside development will encompass group instruction in areas of common need and individual programs decided upon by the manager in consultation with the human resources executive.

In-house training will consist of challenging and varied assignments given according to a predetermined schedule and will include job rotation, job enlargement, special assignments, and task force work.

On-the-job coaching and development will be stressed along with frequent reviews of performance in meeting goals. Salary action and timing of promotions have to be carefully worked out to keep these young people with high potential challenged and interested.

Each development plan will be reviewed and approved initially by managers at the next two higher levels. Additional reviews of progress and salary action will be made every six months by those same executives. Career plans will also be reviewed with each individual to insure that his manager's plans parallel his own plans and are consonant with his needs, interests, abilities, and motivations.

If a division or corporate staff department has no young executives with high potential, the manager will be asked to hire one or two young executives as additions to the payroll or to fill open jobs or to perform significant measurable work or as replacements in important positions. A time limit for these additions should be set at one year.

This program recognizes that management development is an individual process involving the interaction of the man, his job, his manager, and his work environment. Development implies improvement in performance and preparation for advancement through the acquisition of new knowledge, skills, and attitudes. This program should also pinpoint key management manpower strengths and limitations at the same time that it identifies the strengths and limitations of promising young employees.

POSITION DESCRIPTION: COMPANY PRESIDENT

Broad Function: The president is the chief operating officer of the company. He is responsible for operating the company in such manner as to increase the intrinsic value of the common stock through consistent growth in earnings per share and to build a stronger base for continued growth.

Reports to: Chairman and chief executive officer.

Principal Responsibilities:

1. Provide leadership and overall direction in all company activities including the development, production, promotion, and sale of its products to yield optimum short-term profit, while providing for future growth and diversification.
2. Directly supervise the industry group heads and insure that they organize, administer, and control the operations of their groups in a prudent and professional manner, while maintaining an organizational climate which encourages entrepreneurial leadership at operating levels.
3. Provide overall direction to the corporate staff in carrying out its responsibilities.
4. Direct the allocation of capital funds, including the appropriate reviews, approvals, and audits, to yield optimum return on investment.
5. Work closely with the chairman of the board in growth and diversification matters including financing, acquisitions, and mergers.
6. Develop a sound general organization plan and spur the staffing of senior management positions with well-qualified individuals; per-

sonally review and approve (a) all major changes in division organization and (b) personnel actions affecting executives earning more than $35,000 per year.

7. Provide overall direction, including personal periodic review and appraisal, in the preparation and implementation of long-range plans.
8. Review and approve annual division profit plans, monitor performances of all divisions against profit plans, and see that necessary action is taken to realize plan objectives.
9. Insure that systems of control are established as necessary to avoid surprises.
10. Provide the impetus in formulating, implementing, and continually appraising a companywide management development program.
11. Insure that executive incentives and benefits identify the interests of key executives with those of shareowners.
12. Establish and maintain clear and open channels of communication throughout the company and see that information needs are clearly met.
13. See that the company's information system is kept modernized to provide the effective flow of data necessary for proper management control and direction of operations.
14. Regularly report company progress in attaining sales, profit, investment, and growth objectives to the chairman, the executive committee, and the board of directors.
15. Maintain first-hand knowledge of markets, customers, and products by periodic personal visits to key plant locations and major customers.
16. Promote the image of the company among shareowners, employees, and the general public and see that effective public relations programs are properly implemented.
17. Refer matters of major importance, along with recommendations, to the chairman of the board for consultation, approval, or decision.
18. Through monthly meetings with the business policy group, provide for a coordinated management approach throughout the company, reviewing all matters of major concern, including operating problems, major programs before launching, and appraisal of key activities after completion.
19. Serve as a member of the executive committee and the board of directors.

PERSONNEL SPECIFICATIONS: COMPANY PRESIDENT

Age: Preferably 40 to 55 years.

Education: Bachelor's degree and graduate work in business administration.

Experience: Minimum of five years' general management responsibility, preferably in large multiplant manufacturing company with full profit responsibility.

Line and staff multiindustry and multiproduct experience in at least two of the three following functional areas is highly desirable: marketing and sales, manufacturing, finance.

Outstanding record of achievement in sales, profitability, and return on investment as well as in acquisitions and mergers. Company and sales growth record should be in a highly competitive business.

Working knowledge and evidence of application of modern management tools such as business planning, organization planning, management by objectives, financial measurements and controls, information systems, marketing strategy and intelligence, capital investments, and expenditures analysis.

Strong record of outside participation in community and business associations and professional organizations.

Personal Qualifications:

Executive stature including vigor, stamina, high energy level.

Demonstrated initiative, dedication, and commitment.

Demonstrated ability to build an effective team.

Evidence of strong communication skills, both oral and written.

Ability to establish and adhere to priorities which have greatest potential profit impact.

CANDIDATE QUALIFICATION ANALYSIS

Title: President, Subsidiary Company Division: ________

Candidate: John Smith

Personnel Specifications

Age: 40–55 years

Education: BS + graduate work in business administration

Experience: Minimum 5 years of general management responsibility (preferably in large multiplant manufacturing)

Line and staff experience in two of three areas:

Marketing and sales

Manufacturing

Finance

Multiindustry and multiproduct experience

Candidate Qualifications—Factual

Born 8/17/27; 45 years of age

Education: AB + MBA + Harvard AMP

Senior vice president and subsidiary president, 1/69/ to date, 3½ years

Vice president and division general manager, 7/64–1/69, 4½ years

Division general manager, 1962–1964, 2 years

Staff administrative assistant; assistant advertising manager; advertising manager; 1957–1962, 5 years

Salesman; district sales manager; regional sales manager; 1950–1957, 7 years

No direct manufacturing experience; some production control; entire career spent in textiles

CANDIDATE QUALIFICATION ANALYSIS (Continued)

JUDGMENTAL DATA TO BE COMPLETED BY NOMINATING OFFICER

	Judgment					
	0 = Unable to Rate	1 = Outstanding	2 = Superior	3 = Good	4 = Minimum Acceptable	5 = Unsatisfactory
Record of achievement, including:						
1. Growth in sales, profitability, ROI		x				
2. Acquisitions and mergers		x				
Working knowledge and application of management tools and techniques		x				
Record of outside participation in community and business associations and professional organizations			x			
Personal Qualifications						
Executive stature including energy level, health		x				
Initiative, dedication, and commitment		x				
Ability to build effective team			x			
Communication skills, oral and written			x			
Ability to establish and adhere to priorities for greatest potential profit impact			x			

Recommendation

Immediate temporary replacement	Near-term replacement (2–3 years)	Long-term replacement (within 10 years)
		xx

PERFORMANCE APPRAISAL AND REVIEW FORM

Name:____________________________ Corporate/Division:____________________

Title:____________________________ Appraisal date:____________________

Rating: ☐ Outstanding ☐ Excellent ☐ Good ☐ Marginal ☐ Unsatisfactory

---

Major accomplishments (past 12 months):

Areas of underachievement:

Targets for next 12 months, including personal improvement goals:

Review Manager____________________________

Acknowledged________________________ Date____________________________

Personal Résumé
Public Relations and Employee Relations Manpower Inventory (To be completed by employee) *please type*

PHOTO
2″ × 2″

Last Name	First Name	Initial	Date résumé prepared

Present Position	Position Level

Division	Departments	Location

Education (college, university, other)	Course	From	To	Degree

Marital status	Children

Sex	Height	Weight

Military service (branch)	Years	Highest rank	Present status	Continuous service date	Birth date	Birthplace	Citizenship

Work experience including company training programs (begin with present position)

From–To	Company	Nature and scope of work	Position level	Name of supervisor

Company Courses

Year	Course	Year	Course	Year	Course	Year	Course

Specialized Courses

(Military courses, night courses) (College courses not part of above degrees)

Year	Course	Year	Course	Year	Course	Year	Course

Honors and Awards

(Honorary fraternities, degrees, fellowships, managerial awards, publications, etc.)

Year				Year			

Outside Activities

(Business associations, civic and social organizations, sports, hobbies and other interests)

Future

Describe any health factor which must be considered in relation to your placement

Geographical preferences:

Future Work Experience Desires (Rank in Order of Preference)

Community Relations____ Employee Comm.____ Sal. Adminis.____ Communication____ Personnel Develp. & Adminis.____
Education & Trng____ Health & Sfty.____ Union Rltns.____ Educ. Rlts. & Corp. Supp.____ Researeh____
Employee Benefit____ Person. Prctcs.____ Wage Admin.____ Employee Compensa.____ Union Relations____
Function Other Than Public & Employee Relations:____ Investor Relations____

What is your immediate job goal?

What ultimate job goal do you consider yourself capable of?

Comments:

Please review your completed Résumé with your Employee Relations Manager

Employee's Signature	Reviewed by:	Title	Date Submitted

ATTITUDE SURVEY

Representative Questions for Professional Employees

This questionnaire is part of an opinion survey on employee relations practices. *It is not a test. There are no "right" or "wrong" answers.* You are asked to help by contributing your opinion and reaction on the attached questionnaire. Participation on your part is entirely voluntary.

This survey is strictly anonymous. No person who participates in it can be identified. Completed questionnaires will be keypunched and processed through a computer.

Please feel completely free to indicate exactly what you think on each question by checking the *one answer* which most nearly reflects your opinion. *Please do not sign your name.*

Please check (X) appropriate box:
A. ☐ Specialist/individual contributor
B. ☐ Manager

Throughout "your manager" refers to your immediate manager or supervisor

Many factors go to provide job satisfaction. Some are more important than others. Review the following factors and place a check in the appropriate column opposite each one to indicate *how important* it is for you personally.

		1. Very important	2. Quite important	3. Somewhat important	4. Not important
A-1	*Supervisor:* working for a good manager	________	________	________	________
A-2	*Advancement:* having a chance to get a better job	________	________	________	________
A-3	*Pay:* the amount of money I get	________	________	________	________
A-4	*Benefit plans:* insurance, pension, etc.	________	________	________	________
A-5	*Security:* being sure of steady employment	________	________	________	________
A-6	*Type of work:* doing work I like and find interesting	________	________	________	________
A-7	*Personal development:* being able to get education and training	________	________	________	________
A-8	*Appraisal:* knowing what my manager thinks of my performance	________	________	________	________
A-9	*Working conditions:* having adequate equipment, surroundings, etc.	________	________	________	________
A-10	*Company:* working for a company I can be proud of	________	________	________	________
A-11	*Work group:* having a good group to work with	________	________	________	________
A-12	*Communication:* being informed on matters I need to know about	________	________	________	________

Now that you have indicated how important these factors are to you, please indicate *how satisfactory* you consider each factor to be at present.

		Very satis-factory	Satis-factory	Not satis-factory	Quite unsatis-factory
B-1	*Supervisor:* working for a good manager	______	______	______	______
B-2	*Advancement:* having a chance to get a better job	______	______	______	______
B-3	*Pay:* the amount of money I get	______	______	______	______
B-4	*Benefit plans:* insurance, pension, etc.	______	______	______	______
B-5	*Security:* being sure of steady employment	______	______	______	______
B-6	*Type of work:* doing work I like and find interesting	______	______	______	______
B-7	*Personal development:* being able to get education and training	______	______	______	______
B-8	*Appraisal:* knowing what my manager thinks of my performance	______	______	______	______
B-9	*Working conditions:* having adequate equipment, surroundings, etc.	______	______	______	______
B-10	*Company:* working for a company I can be proud of	______	______	______	______
B-11	*Work group:* having a good group to work with	______	______	______	______
B-12	*Communication:* being informed on matters I need to know about	______	______	______	______

Appendix B Hourly Rated Employees

Hourly Rated Employee Forms

Engagement Record (a multi-purpose form designed for computer applications—replaced 16 separate pieces of paper)
Computerized Record System for Hourly Rated Employees
Planned Advancement Procedure
Planned Advancement Register

ENGAGEMENT RECORD

DATE PREPARED

PERSONAL DATA

Employee Ident. No.	000	________	Unit	002	________
Name (Last, First, Initial)	004	________	Name Suffix	005	________
Street Address (1st Line)	245	________			
Street Address (2nd Line)	261	________			
City, State and Zip Code	277	________	Soc. Sec. No.	003	________
Phone Number	286	________	Birth Date	006	________
Sex	008	____M ____F	Marital Status	009	____M ____S
Height	278	____Ft. ____In.	Weight	279	____Lbs.
Patent Agreement	010	____Y ____N	Fidelity Bond	011	____Y ____N

EDUCATION

Training Program	118	________	College Initial Degree	119	________
Course Initial Degree	120	________	Year of Graduation Initial Degree	121	________
College Highest Post Graduate Degree	122	________	Course Highest Post Graduate Degree	123	________
Highest Post Graduate Degree	124	________	Number Years School	280	________

POSITION DATA

Type of Engagement	202	New	__11	Re-Engage	__12 __13 __14		Transfer	__17		
Type Worker	176	Exempt	__1	Non-Ex-Sal	__2	Hourly Direct	__3	Hourly Indirect	__4	
Method of Payment	175	Bi-Weekly	__B	Weekly	__W	Hourly Incentive	__P	Hourly Day Work	__D	Casual __C

JOB NO. POSITION TITLE

Field	Code	Entry	Field	Code	Entry
Job No. and Position Title	039	________			
Account No.	020	________	Temp. or Prov. Level	109	________
Continuity of Service Date	007	________	Seniority Date	260	________
Record Status	174	Active ___1 Casual ___7	Regular Scheduled Hours	173	________ (XX.X)
Paid Level	042	________	Hourly Rate	023	________(XX.XXXX)
Job Level	037	________	Weekly Rate	024	________ (XXX.XX)
Job Family No.	411	________	Annual Rate	045	________ (XXXXX.)
Shift (027)	281	___1st ___2nd ___3rd	Medical Code	295	___A ___B ___C
Effective Date	038-040-043-203	________	Examination Year	294	________

PAY DATA

Field	Code	Entry	Field	Code	Entry
PENSION STATUS	032	________	CHARITY DED. CODE	078	________
INS. EMPLOYEE	025	________	CHARITY DED. METHOD	079	____Fixed ____Percent
INS. DEPENDENT	026	________	CHARITY DED.	080	________ (XX.XX)
STOCK BONDS DED.	050	________ (XXX.XX)	BARGAINING GROUP	081	________
REGULAR BOND DED.	056	________ (XXX.XX)	BARGAINING DUES DED.	082	___Yes ___No
WH/TAX EXEMPTIONS	072	________ (XX)	SAVINGS PLAN	046	________
WH/TAX ADDIT. DED.	073	________ (XXX.XX)	NON-PROGRAM ADDER	172	________1
STATE & LOCAL TAX CODE	092	________	TIME REPORTING BASIS	177	________
TAX STATUS	093	___Y Active___ N Inactive	INS. RISK CLASS	149	________
MARITAL STATUS	094	________	STATE OF RESIDENCE	017	________
% GROSS SUBJECT	096	________	STATE & CITY CODE	018	________
			NO. DEPENDENTS	095	________
			OPTIONAL ADD. DED.	097	________ (XX.XX)

COMPUTERIZED RECORD FOR HOURLY EMPLOYEES

NAME	PHONE	C/S DATE	SENIORITY

BIRTH DATE	SOCIAL SECURITY	PAY NO.

ADDRESS	WEEKLY RATE	ED.	MAINT.	SEN.	DUES	BARGAIN UNIT

UNIT	DATE ASSIGNED	POSITION TITLE	JOB #	JOB FAMILY	PAID C #	JOB C #	SHIFT	TYPE
XXX							X	
XXX							X	

DATES OF LAYOFF	DATES OF RECALL	REMOVAL FROM PAYROLL	REASON FOR JOB CHANGE	
				MEDICAL CODE ___
		LAST DAY WORKED ___	___ REDUCTION	EXAM YEAR ___
			___ UPGRADING	SEX ___
		EFFECTIVE DATE ___	___ NOT QUAL.	HEIGHT ___
		PAY THROUGH ___	___ PHYSICAL	WEIGHT ___
		DAYS VACATION PAY ___	___ TRANSFER	NEW EMPL. ___
			___ OTHER	CO. TRANSFER ___
		REASON ___ REHIRE ___		REENGAGED ___

PLANNED ADVANCEMENT PROCEDURE FOR HOURLY EMPLOYEES

The company recognizes the desirability of utilizing the greatest skill possessed by its employees and of giving employees the opportunity for promotion. Therefore, when a vacancy occurs within the bargaining unit, after qualified employees within a department have had a chance to consider the vacancy, a new planned advancement procedure will be followed. Under this new procedure, any employee, except probationary employees, may apply for a higher-rated job classification at any time and will not risk missing a promotion if he is absent because of verified personal illness or vacation for a period not to exceed four weeks. The new procedure will operate as follows.

1. Lists of all current job classifications will be placed with foremen, supervisors, and the personnel department. These lists will identify all jobs in the plant. As a new job classification is established, notices will be placed on the bulletin boards so that planned advancement register applications may be made by interested employees.

2. To apply for an upgrading within the bargaining unit, an employee will obtain an application form from his foreman and fill it out completely, listing the classification and shift desired. This expression of shift choice is no guarantee that it will be granted; the contract provides that "employees with the most seniority shall have shift preference." Employees may apply for a reasonable number of jobs by completing an application for each job desired.

3. To be considered eligible for an available upgrading, an employee must have his application already on file on the date that personnel is notified of such an opening. Employees may properly request any classification that would constitute upgrading, but applications may be considered for shift transfers and lateral or downward transfers where there is good cause for such. These latter applications will be honored only where no eligible employees have applied. Probationary employees are ineligible to apply in all cases.

4. The company will review all applications for a given opening and select an employee who, in its judgment, has the necessary qualifications. In making this determination it will use the same selection techniques used in determining the qualifications of nonemployees. However, in selecting the employee, seniority will be a factor. Where seniority is the deciding factor, selection will be made from among applicants within the seniority area; if no qualified applicants exist in the area, the selection will be based upon total plant seniority.

In case of dispute, the company will not be required to give any employee a trial period on the job to determine his qualifications.

If no fully qualified employee has applied for a particular job, the company will have the right to hire a new employee for the vacancy.

5. If an employee refuses a job when it is offered, his application will be voided and he will not be eligible to reapply for the same classification for a period of six months.

6. Employees accepting upgrading will be ineligible for further upgrades for a period of twelve months.

7. The company will be free to fill openings on a temporary basis with any employee qualified, in its opinion, without incurring any liability to any employee finally selected as a result of this planned advancement procedure.

Planned Advancement Register for Hourly Employees

(Please print all data on this form—all questions must be answered)

Employee's name______________________________Seniority date__________

Clock #______________Age______Height______Weight______Unit______

I. POSITION DESIRED

____________	____________	____________	____________
Job Title	Job #	Shift	"C" Rate

II. QUALIFICATIONS

____________	____________	____________	____________
Present Job Title	Job #	Shift	"C" Rate

EDUCATION—TRAINING

1. Circle highest grade

GRAMMAR SCHOOL	HIGH SCHOOL	COLLEGE
1 2 3 4 5 6 7 8	9 10 11 12	13 14 15 16

College Major__________Minor__________

2. List high school shop training or other courses completed which may help qualify you for the position desired.

______	______	______	______	______	______
Course	Semesters	Course	Semesters	Course	Semesters

3. List other technical training (trade school—night school—correspondence courses—military service—apprentice training programs)

____________	____________	____________
Subject	Length of Training Program	Source of Training
____________	____________	____________
Subject	Length of Training Program	Source of Training

Can you read blueprints? ____Yes____No

Can you read precision instruments? ____Yes____No List instruments you can read

____

4. Have you had work experience with other employers in the position to which you seek advancement? Yes____No____. If yes, indicate below:

From_______To______Employer__________________Type of work__________

From_______To______Employer__________________Type of work__________

5. Have you ever performed this work with this company?_____Yes_____No

When?__________________In what unit?__________________

Supervisor's signature______________________________Date__________

Index